D1478798

The Coach's Devotional

Marty Mayer

The Coach's Devotional

Cross Training Publishing
www.crosstrainingpublishing.com
(308) 293-3891
Copyright © 2017 by Marty Mayer
ISBN: 978-1-938254-72-7

Foreword

"He has a gift with words!"

My director within FCA, Aaron Hogue, said those words to me after reading an email Marty had sent to a list of nearly 100 coaches he had been speaking life into for years.

I completely agree. Marty does have a gift with words and more specifically a gift of encouraging coaches just like you. I believe God uses him so powerfully in this way because for decades he has been in your shoes.

At 71 years old Marty is still coaching, now as a volunteer with the track team at Northern Kentucky University. Even though he is well into retirement age, you can sometimes see him getting in a run on the streets of the NKU campus.

When he is not coaching his own athletes, you will likely find him taking time to give a coach a listening ear, a timely word of wisdom, and a feeling they are loved by their Father in heaven more than they can ever imagine.

To the best of our ability we've bottled up this gift Marty has given to coaches into this book for you. Wisdom, understanding, and an encouragement to connect with your Father in heaven will be on every page.

We know you don't have a lot of time on your hands. That is why this book is jam packed with life-giving "quick hits" from God's Word. Marty takes all sorts of sports analogies and creates a memorable way to learn and remember important life lessons.

Marty has been a blessing to my own spiritual growth, my marriage, family, and ministry. My prayer is that this book will bless you as well.

It is possible to win on the scoreboard and in life. This man has done it. Open your eyes and heart to the following pages because Marty is in your corner.

Nate Sallee
Area Director
Northern Kentucky FCA

Introduction

I never intended for these devotionals to be more than weekly emails of encouragement to coaches. Beginning in 2012, I sat down either Monday or Tuesday of most weeks at a computer in the local library and composed what you are about to read. The subject line of the weekly emails simply read "encouragement." I drew the athletic content of the emails from almost 30 years of coaching track and field at Bellevue High School, a small class A school in Northern Kentucky, set two blocks from the banks of the Ohio River, coupled with my first 22 years of life growing up in the football-rich state of Texas along with a deep desire to help us all apply God's Word to our lives.

Sometime in 2016, several staff members of the Fellowship of Christian Athletes suggested I compile these weekly emails and submit them for publication. Not being very computer savvy, I asked, "How do I do that?" They told me that all I had to do was go to my "sent" box of emails and upload them to a file. The prospect of finding those emails seemed overwhelming. I might as well have been told to go run back-to-back marathons. (I have never even run one!) However, a very kind lady by the name of Cindy Fessler understood perfectly what had to be done and uploaded them to a file we called "Marty's encouragements." The journey had begun.

Thanks to Gordon Thiessen for giving this rookie the ball and helping him get past the line of scrimmage to follow the blocks of helpful editors and find his way to the end zone of publication.

Thanks to my dear wife, Bobbie, for over 37 years of encouraging me so I could encourage others. If a star fell from heaven each time I thought of her, the sky would be empty.

I hope you are blessed as you read these "encouragements" and allow God to use His Word in your life.

Strength in the Battle

Goal line stands provide some of a football game's most memorable moments. The defense has been driven down the field, and here they are, their backs to the goal line. To turn back the offense would be a huge victory. To allow them to take the last few feet of turf and score would be defeat. It is time to take a stand. The crowd is roaring! Both sides are lined up for the snap.

A goal line stand is an exciting moment in sports, but in the game of life it can be a challenging moment, especially if you are the one with your back to the goal line and looking at the possibility of the enemy scoring a major victory in your life. He has driven you the length of the field, and here you are.

"He will be a spirit of justice to him who sits in judgment, a source of strength to those who turn back the battle at the gate." (Isaiah 28:6)

"Seek the Lord and His strength; seek His face continually." (Psalm 105:4)

God wants to give you strength when your back is to the goal line of life (similar to the gates of the city in ancient times.) The goal line may be relational, financial, emotional, or spiritual. God wants to strengthen you to turn back the battle at the goal line.

Lord, turn back the battle raging in my life. I look to You for strength.

Discussion:

1. Describe a memorable goal line stand from your coaching experience. Maybe your team was down in a match or a runner way behind in a race.

2. Have you ever had your back to the goal line in your personal life? How did you respond?

The Coaches' Office

Some coaches' office doors have a sign on them reading "Coaches Only." Athletes stay in the locker room. Coaches stay in their office. No mix.

When Jesus was crucified "the curtain of the temple was torn in two from top to bottom." (Mark 15:38) That curtain separated the Holy Place from the Holy of Holies. Only one person ever entered the Holy of Holies, and that was the high priest, and he entered only once a year. Pretty exclusive!

Not anymore! When Jesus was crucified, the wall of separation was ripped in two. Now everyone has access, not just a special few. That means you and I can now come into God's presence because Jesus made a way.

Next time you go into your coach's office, remember Jesus ripped that "door" right off the hinges. No more separation. I am not suggesting you shouldn't have a door on your coach's office! It's just an encouragement to remember the cross.

Lord, thank You for access to You through the cross. No time limit to our meeting. No standing in line. Thank You that you take me just as I am: sweaty, irritated, excited. What an awesome privilege to come into Your presence at a moment's notice. I am just your assistant coach!

Discussion:

1. Who are some of the most intimidating coaches you have played for as an athlete or coached with as a peer? What made them seem that way?

2. What makes a coach "approachable" to his players?

Hard Workouts

8 X 400 in 65 with a two-minute rest sounds painful, unless you remember the reason you are doing it . . . to get to the state meet! Standing on the award stand at the state meet will make all those hard workouts worthwhile. We endure now for a reward later.

"Let us fix our eyes on Jesus, the author, and perfecter of our faith, who for the joy set before him endured the cross, scorning its shame, and sat down at the right hand of the throne of God." (Hebrews 12:1-2)

Part of what got Jesus through the agony of the cross was that He never turned his eyes away from the joy of soon being able to sit down at His Father's right hand, his work on earth completed. Jesus was able to endure the torture of the cross because He anticipated a later reward.

When we lose our "why," we lose our way.

Lord, give me endurance. Keep my eyes on You and not on the circumstances of my life. No matter how good it gets or how bad it gets, keep me looking at the cross.

Discussion:

1. Describe one of the hardest workouts you ever did as an athlete?

2. Describe one of the hardest workouts you ever had your athletes do?

3. What have been some of "life's hard workouts" for you in your personal life?

Preparation for Giants

The sign hung on the wall—Perfect practice makes perfect. Hours in the weight room precede only seconds of actual competition; the shot putter spins in the circle and explodes at the front of the circle, or a lineman drives his opponent off the line of scrimmage.

A page in a sports magazine showed a runner running in front of empty stands. The accompanying quote said, "The real heroics take place when the stadium is empty."

We all know David slew the giant Goliath, but we may not know that before this historic battle, David was a lonely shepherd on the rocky, rolling hills of Israel. However, in those days by himself, David learned to protect his sheep. "When a lion or a bear came and carried off a sheep from the flock, I went after it, struck it and rescued the sheep from its mouth. When it turned on me, I seized it by its hair, struck it and killed it." 1 Samuel 17:34-35

David's days as a lonely shepherd prepared him for the great battle with Goliath. Lots of preparation for a five-minute encounter.

Lord, prepare me well for the time I am called up. That may be at home tonight or at practice tomorrow. Help me perform the small tasks well even though they go unnoticed. Keep me filling up the Gatorade cooler. Maybe some day it will be poured over my head!

Discussion:

1. What is the longest period you have been an assistant? Head coach?

2. If you are a head coach, describe why that role is what you always wanted.

3. What are you hoping to learn as an assistant that will help when you become a head coach?

Strikeout Pitches

Every pitcher has his strikeout pitch: a fastball, a wicked curveball that makes the batter look foolish, a slider, or maybe a changeup that upsets the batter's timing.

The world has its version of strikeout pitches, not mistakes that put you off the team but events that send you back to the dugout with the bat on your shoulders.

"Do not love the world or anything in the world. If anyone loves the world, the love of the Father is not in him. For everything in the world- the cravings of the flesh, the lust of the eyes, and the boasting of what he has and does—comes not from the Father but from the world." (1 John 2:15-16)

There are many nasty pitches, including extreme sexual cravings, longing for more and better stuff, and bragging about what we have or what we have accomplished. They tempt us, and if we are not careful, will strike us out and send us back to the bench.

If you have swung at some of these pitches as I have, it is always good to know that God gives another chance at bat. He is a gracious, forgiving coach.

Lord, I feel I live my life with two strikes against me most of the day. I have struck out so many times before. I think I may have set a school record for strike-outs! Keep me from swinging at everything offered to me. Give me a good eye and a good heart.

Discussion:

1. Which of the three "strikeout pitches" listed in 1 John 2:15-16 do you struggle with the most?

2. Share a time God sent you back to "the dugout."

3. Romans 5:20 says, "Where sin abounded, grace abounded all the more." Share a time grace abounded in your life?

Don't Look

In the 1980's Carl Lewis was running the 100-meter dash against Ben Johnson, the heralded sprinter from Canada. Lewis was running well until Ben Johnson made a surge and Carl Lewis made a mistake, one that cost him the race. He turned his head and looked at Johnson. Not only did he look once; he looked twice. Johnson won. Lewis was second.

"Therefore since we are surrounded by such a great cloud of witnesses, let us throw off everything that hinders us and the sin that so easily entangles us and let us run with perseverance the race set before us. Let us fix our eyes on Jesus, the author and perfecter of our faith..." (Hebrews 12: 1-2)

Looking at other runners in a race can prove to be disastrous. Looking at other people, perhaps other coaches who are more successful and seem to be surging in their careers, can be harmful too.

Lord, keep me from looking at the guy beside me. Help me to know I can't control him. Keep me looking down the track at the finish line. Stop me from gloating over those who may be behind me or jealous of those ahead of me.

Discussion:

1. Describe some situations where you have been envious of another coach?

2. What causes you to envy others and compare yourself to other coaches?

3. What could we do to help keep us from looking at the other runners in life?

Disqualification

Bang! Bang! Two shots from the starter's gun. If you are a track coach and have an athlete in the race, your stomach just entered the knot tying contest. That second shot means only one thing - a false start and disqualification. Hopefully not your runner. There is no sadder sight than seeing a disqualified runner pick up his or her sweats and walk off the track.

The apostle Paul knew the distinct possibility of being disqualified himself.

"Do you not know that in a race all the runners run, but only one gets the prize? Run in such a way as to get the prize. Everyone who competes in the games goes into strict training. They do it to get a crown that will not last, but we do it to get a crown that will last forever. Therefore I do not run like a man running aimlessly; I do not fight like a man beating the air. No, I beat my body and make it my slave so that after I have preached to others, I myself should not be disqualified from the prize." (1 Corinthians 9:24-27)

One thing Paul was afraid of was that he would be disqualified from the race of ministering to others. That took a lot of determination and discipline. Paul wasn't a recreational runner; he was doing all he could to win.

Lord, keep me in the race. Help me exercise self-control in the little things: the looks, my thoughts, that sarcastic remark. Keep me mindful of the prize.

Discussion:

1. Do you recall witnessing or being the coach of a runner who was disqualified in a race?

2. How do you think the disqualified athlete felt? What was going on in their head?

3. What is the prize Paul speaks of in the above verse?

Finisher

Allyson Felix was almost dead last coming off the curve in the finals of the 400 meters at the Olympic Trials in 2016, but by the time she reached the finish line she was in first place. Allyson Felix is a finisher.

". . . being confident of this, that he who began a good work in you will carry it on to completion until the day of Christ Jesus." (Philippians 1:6)

God is always at work. He finishes what He begins. If He starts the race, He will finish it. He is at work from the opening kickoff of your relationship with Him to the very last tick of the clock of the fourth quarter; during the timeouts, halftime, and even during the turnovers. God is always at work.

Lord, thank You that you are always at work in our lives. Help me believe that even when I fumble the ball, and even when I stumble in the race. Thank you that You will finish what You begin.

Discussion:

1. Share a time when you felt like you had turned the ball over in your life?

2. What are some projects you began that either you did not finish or had a hard time finishing? What caused you to falter?

3. What is your response to the fact that God is always at work in your life?

The Blame Game

It was the second fumble of the first quarter on the same type of exchange. The quarterback and halfback walked off the field yelling and pointing their fingers at each other.

The first game to ever be played was the blame game. Adam and Eve played it a long time ago when Adam blamed Eve for eating the fruit. Adam played the game, but he lost the unity with his wife. The same thing can happen with a team. Blaming can destroy the unity of any team.

"And God said, "Who told you that you were naked? Have you eaten from the tree that I commanded you not to eat from?" The man said, 'The woman you put here with me-she gave me some of the fruit from the tree, and I ate it." (Genesis 3:11-12)

As coaches, we can blame our assistants or players. As spouses, we blame our spouse or our kids. Players can blame other players and coaches. Adam could have stepped up when Satan made his offer to Eve, but he didn't say anything.

Coaches, the blame game is easy to play, but when you do, everybody loses.

Lord, keep me from playing the blame game in my heart, from blaming myself to blaming my assistants or players or the gang at home. Stop me from condemning others because they fail to meet my expectations, which keeps me from feeling good about myself. Stop me from depending on others for my worth, rather than You. I thank you that You love me, regardless of my performance. Help me behave the same way toward others on my team.

Discussion:

1. Describe a time you blamed someone else for a bad play or something that reflected poorly on you.

2. Share a time someone blamed you for a mistake or poor play? How did it make you feel? Can you still recall that emotion today?

Credentials

A football coach in Texas had quite a list of credentials: born during halftime of the Texas-Oklahoma football game to parents who were both All-American, coached three state championship football teams and set a Texas state record for career victories. He is now a pastor of a small church in rural west Texas.

The apostle Paul had a similar list of credentials regarding his religious standing in the community. However, he says the following at the end of that list.

"But whatever was to my profit, I now consider loss for the sake of Christ. What is more I consider everything a loss in view of the surpassing value of knowing Christ Jesus my Lord for whom I have suffered the loss of all things in order that I may gain Christ." (Philippians 4:7-8)

Paul was a great religious figure in his day. However, in comparison to knowing Jesus, his credentials seemed to him like nothing. His relationship with Jesus was so important that it made everything else pale in comparison.

Lord, help me keep my relationship with You always in view. May my successes never surpass the value of simply knowing You.

Discussion:

1. Describe some great achievements in your coaching career.

2. How does knowing Christ compare to those achievements?

3. Is Paul saying there is something wrong with great achievements? Why or why not?

Practice

"Whatever you have learned or received or heard from me, or seen in me put into practice. And the God of peace will be with you." (Philippians 4:9)

Going to clinics in the spring or summer gives us a lot of great ideas, but putting them into practice may be a little harder. Unless an idea translates from paper to practice it is not very practical.

Our time with God is much the same. Reading God's Word is like going to a clinic; putting that information into practice is the tough part. Sometimes it takes a lot of reps to get something right.

One of the practice sessions I struggle with most takes place right in my own home. A verse in I Corinthians says that love "does not take into account a wrong suffered." I am pretty good at taking things into account when I feel like I have been wronged, so I need lots of practice to get that attitude right.

Lord, help me be ready for the hard practices. Stop me from keeping track of the wrongs I have suffered. Help me throw away my scorecard and just give grace to people.

Discussion:

1. Who is one of the best clinic speakers you have ever heard? What made him/her so impactful?

2. What are some attitudes or actions from God's Word that you feel you need to put into practice?

A Winning Formation

Coaches, below is a winning roster for life:

• **Center**: Center your life on Jesus. ". . . in Him all things hold together." (Colossians 1:17)

• **Guard**: Guard your heart. "Above all else, guard your heart, for it influences everything else in your life." (Proverbs 4:23)

• **Tackle**: Tackle your thoughts. ". . . and we take every thought captive to make it obey Christ." (2 Corinthians 10:5)

• **Tight end**: End negativity. "Finally, brothers, whatever is true, whatever is noble, whatever is right, whatever is pure, whatever is lovely, whatever is admirable—if anything is excellent or praiseworthy—think about such things." (Philippians 4:8)

• **Receiver**: Receive all God has for you every day. "Because of the Lord's great love we are not consumed, for his compassions never fail. They are new every morning; great is His faithfulness." (Lamentations 3:22-23)

• **Linebacker**: Back up your coaches and athletes with encouragement. "Let no unwholesome word come out of your mouth but only what is helpful for building others up according to their needs, that it may benefit those who listen." (Ephesians 4:29)

Lord, may I fill all these positions by your grace. Help me be a good teammate on the field and in my home.

Discussion:

1. Who is the best player you have ever seen at one of these positions?

2. Which of these positions is the easiest for you to accomplish?

3. Which of these positions is the hardest for you to accomplish?

The Colors

When a football team takes the field on Friday night, they all wear the same colored jersey. When a cross country team steps to the starting line on Saturday morning, they all wear the same colored singlet. When a soccer team takes the field, they all wear the school uniform.

When Christ-followers take the field of life, they all wear the same colors, but this jersey covers our heart and then makes its way into our behavior. Inwardly real. Outwardly apparent.

"Therefore, as God's chosen people, holy and dearly loved, clothe yourselves with compassion, kindness, humility, gentleness, and patience." (Colossians 3:12)

Lord, may I suit up with You on my heart in the same way my team puts on a uniform for the contest. May I wear the colors of Your heart on mine tonight.

Discussion:

1. Which of these team colors in Colossians 3:12 is a bit faded in your life?

2. What is the most colorful uniform you have ever noticed? What school wore it?

The Grand Marshal

Homecoming parades are exciting events! At the front of all the floats and convertibles carrying hopeful kings and queens is the Grand Marshal of the parade. The grand marshal is usually a former teacher, player or coach who loves every minute of waving to the crowd. I got to be a grand marshal after I retired; I threw out a lot of candy in the ten blocks from the firehouse to the stadium!

The Bible talks about another parade and another grand marshal. This parade is the parade of life, and Jesus is the grand marshal.

"Thanks be to God, who always leads us in His triumph in Christ..." (2 Corinthians 2:14) This verse refers to times when conquering kings return leading their captives through the city streets.

The times I struggle the most are those when I try to be the grand marshal myself. My little parade is always getting lost and can't seem to find the stadium. I am much better off to let Jesus sit in the convertible and follow Him.

Lord, I want You to be the grand marshal of my life. I am just glad to be in the parade of Your victory over Satan. You lead. I will follow.

Discussion:

1. Have you ever been the grand marshal of a parade?

2. Describe the most memorable parade you have ever seen.

3. Describe a time when you tried to be the grand marshal of your life.

Yellow Flags

Yellow flags on green grass. Not the best sight on Friday night. Second down and ten is now second and long.

Sometimes God throws a yellow flag on the field of our hearts. Perhaps we were impatient with a player or we were not very understanding of our wife after we got home an hour late and the fish sticks were a little cold!

What happens to a Friday night yellow flag? The referee picks it up and puts it back into his pocket.

Similarly, being honest with God about our mess-ups places the flag back in Jesus' pocket.

"If we confess our sins, He is faithful to forgive us our sins and to cleanse us from all unrighteousness." (1 John 1:9)

Lord, keep picking up the flags of the penalties against me as I confess those things to You. May that flag not stay on the ground too long. Help me be quick and honest to respond to Your calls.

Discussion:

1. Describe a penalty you remember that was a game changer.

2. Is there anything in your life right now that might cause God to throw His yellow flag?

3. Take a minute and pray. Tell God about what caused the yellow flag to come out. Repent of that attitude or action and ask God to forgive you and put that flag back in His pocket.

Savers and the Savior

Sergio Romo, San Francisco Giants. Aroldis Chapman, New York Yankees. Closers. Savers. Their sole responsibility is to preserve or guard from loss (Webster's Dictionary definition of "save"). If they fail in their role, there is a good chance the other team will win.

Two thousand years ago another Saver became a Savior. He did it not by stepping onto a mound, hurling 100+ mph fastballs, and striking out the opposition; He did it by being nailed to a cross and dying for our sins.

 "But when the kindness and love of God our Savior appeared, He saved us, not because of righteous things we had done, but because of His mercy." (Titus 2:4-5)

 Every baseball team has a saver. However, there is only one Savior. I am glad that His death struck out the side and preserved me from tremendous loss.

Jesus, thank you for saving me. Thank you for closing the game against all of Satan's accusations toward me and striking Him out on the cross.

Discussion:

1. Who, in your opinion, is one of the greatest closers in the game of baseball?

2. What attitudes or actions do you see Jesus striking out in your life?

A Long Way to Go

The ball on your own two-yard line; one minute to drive the length of the field and score. Your season on the line. There's not much time remaining and a whole lot at stake. Mission impossible!

Mary may have felt that same sense of expectation mingled with fear when the angel Gabriel showed up in her little house in a small village in Israel and told her she would be the mother of a little boy who would be the Savior of the world.

" 'How will this be,' Mary asked the angel . . . ?" (Luke 1:34)

"How are we going to get from the two-yard line to the opposite goal line, 98 yards away?"

The angel answers Mary the same way he would answer us when we face life's impossibilities: "The Holy Spirit will come upon you, and the power of the Most High will overshadow you." (Luke 1:35)

In less than three minutes during her conversation with the angel Gabriel, Mary moves from fear to faith. May it be the same for us, whatever we are facing on the field, in our classrooms, or in our homes. May "the Holy Spirit come upon you, and the power of the Most High overshadow you" today.

Lord, when the impossible shows up today may I remember what You told Mary. As unlikely as it was that she would give birth to a son without sexual union with a man, may I see You as the God of the impossibilities of my life. I want to live today in the shadow of Your Spirit.

Discussion:

1. Have you ever come from behind to win in the last 60 seconds of a game?

2. Share a time off the field when you felt God showed up during the last minute.

The Scoreboard

I wonder what the scoreboard would look like if God were keeping track of my bad stuff throughout the day, like when I'm snippy with my wife, being sarcastic toward a player, or inwardly smiling when I hear the team of a coach I don't care for got drilled last Friday.

See what this verse from Isaiah 43 says about God's scoreboard.

"I, even I, am He who blots out your transgressions, for my own sake, and remembers your sins no more." (verse 25)

When Jesus died on the cross, He turned off the scoreboard. Sin paid in full. Scoreboard off. Grace on.

The next time you walk into a stadium or a gym, look up at the scoreboard and remind yourself of the awesome forgiveness of God, just for you.

Lord, thanks for turning off the scoreboard of my sin by dying on the cross for me. I am grateful to play this game of life not having to look up at the scoreboard and see yet another mark against me. Scoreboard off. Grace on!

Discussion:

1. Share the last time you did or thought something that would have made it to the scoreboard?

2. When was a time you felt forgiven?

Wrong Goal!

One of my FCA friends told me of the time he inadvertently found himself shooting at the other team's goal during a middle school basketball game. The sad thing was that his cousin on the opposing team kept trying to block his shot! All this despite fans of both teams yelling instructions to both of them!

The game of life can get pretty fast-paced at times, and it is easy to become disoriented. We find ourselves at the wrong goal, trying desperately to make a shot which would only score points for the opposing team.

We need God's Word to get our bearings and get us headed toward the right basket.

"Listen, my son, to a father's instruction; pay attention and gain understanding." (Proverbs 4:1)

Lord, keep me focused on the goal. Stop me from becoming so disoriented that I even forget which way I am heading. Keep my eyes on You; I know I will be headed in the right direction then.

Discussion:

1. Describe a time when someone made a basket or scored points for the other team?

2. How do we score points for the wrong team in life?

3. Have you done that recently? Read this verse out loud: 1 John 1:9: "If we confess our sins God is faithful and righteous to forgive us our sins and cleanse us from all unrighteousness."

On the Field. In the Pressbox

During the game, football coaches need perspective. The field is long, and coaches roam between the 30-yard lines. However, a coach up in the press box has a superior view. He can see what the coach on the field cannot.

The coach on the sidelines has contact with the players. Both the coach in the press box and the coach on the sidelines are necessary. One has perspective. One has contact.

I found this verse in 2 Chronicles interesting regarding one of the great kings of Israel, Hezekiah.

"In everything that he undertook in the service of God's temple and in obedience to the law and the commands, He sought His God and worked wholeheartedly. And so he prospered." (2 Chronicles 31:21)

Working wholeheartedly is an excellent way to play the game of football and a great way to play the game of life. Connected to God in the press box and working hard on the field. Both executed at the same time.

Lord, keep me connected with You and connected with people. Stop me from taking off the headset and going my way. Press box first. Sideline second.

Discussion:

1. In your walk with God, is it easier to stay connected to God through prayer and Bible study or work and serve?

2. What is one thing you could do to help strengthen your weaker area of the two?

What if…?

One of the things coaches are sometimes good at besides coaching (and driving the bus!) is worrying. I used to sit at the table in the morning when I was coaching, and instead of reading my Bible or praying, I was thinking about today's workout or the last devastating injury.

"Who will start if Johnny isn't ready? What if they press us the whole game? I wonder if Sally will be eligible this week?"

Worries sometimes just swarm in our brain like bees in a hive. God understands those concerns.

"Look at the birds of the air; they do not sow or reap or store away in barns, and yet your heavenly Father feeds them. Are you not much more valuable than they? And who of you by worrying can able a single hour to his life? (Matthew 6:26)

You don't see birds at the grocery store walking the aisles! God takes care of them, and you are more valuable than the birds. God wants to take care of us, too, along with our worries.

Right now what is worrying you? Take a moment and pray. Tell God what is bothering you and invite Him into the mix. Maybe He will give you just the wisdom you need for today's practice!

Lord, so much to think about. I do worry. Help me instead to trust You for the things that make me worry. Help me trust You for the things way beyond my control. Care for me like You care for the birds.

Discussion:

1. Share some of the things you seem to worry about the most?

2. Has worry ever helped you solve your problems?

NASCAR with God

NASCAR. Ever been to a NASCAR race? I hadn't either until last Tuesday when I was on my way to church to speak. A lady cut in front of me on the onramp by the Party Source store in Bellevue. The flag went down, and I was six inches off her bumper with a little toot on my horn to let her know I was aware of her maneuver. Yes, I was on my way to church to speak.

In real NASCAR races, not like my Bellevue version, the cars are unbelievably close to each other. Only inches separate the back bumper of one from the front bumper of another.

Maybe God wants us to be that close to Him and other fellow driv ers in the race of life with a better attitude than I had toward cut-off Kate!

James 4:8 says, "Draw near to God, and He will draw near to you..." Stay close to God.

Next time you see a NASCAR race on TV, or you get cut off on the freeway, may it remind you to get close to God. Right on His bumper!

Lord, first forgive me for getting angry with that lady for cutting me off, but do help me stay close to You. You lead. I will follow.

Discussion:

1. Recall the last time you were cut off in traffic. How did you feel?

2. What are some things you do that will help you stay close to God?

Performance

Selection Sunday is always a big day for NCAA basketball! Many players and fans sit on the edge of their seats, waiting to see who will be "in" and who will be left out.

The NCAA selection committee had a hard job, but basically, their selections were based on one thing, performance. Probably no team with a 4-25 record is going to make it unless they win their conference tournament!

Fortunately for us, God doesn't use the same scale.

"For by grace are you saved through faith and that not of yourselves; it is a gift of God, not of works, that no one should boast." (Ephesians 2:8-9)

God chooses us by His grace, not by our performance, good or bad. We may feel like we are a 25-4 person or a 4-25 person. Either way, performance is not the issue. Grace gets us into the tournament. All we have to do is ask. Give Him a call.

Lord, thank You for choosing me by grace and not by my performance as a person or a coach. Thank You for Your mercy, not giving me what I deserve and Your grace, giving me what I don't deserve.

Discussion:

1. Share the story of a game you watched where the underdog won.

2. If you were to give yourself a year-end record based on your performance yesterday, what would it be?

3. Would you like to play any of your real-life games again? Which ones? Why?

Come from Behind

Come-from-behind wins. Down after 24 minutes. Ahead after 48! Down, but not out. A lot of fans counted you out, but in the end you won.

Maybe Jesus knew something of that come-from-behind feeling when He walked out of the tomb. Dead on Friday. Alive on Sunday.

"The angel said to the women, 'Do not be afraid, for I know that you are looking for Jesus, who was crucified. He is not here; he has risen, just as He said . . . " (Matthew 28:5-6)

Not here. Dead people live in tombs. Jesus is not dead!

As you watch the next game or race or match when a team comes from behind to win, remember Jesus came from behind, way behind, to walk out of an empty tomb. Just for you.

Lord, thanks for coming out of a dark grave, for coming from death into life so that I can have life today, even at school on the field and in my home. Keep me from giving up when I feel behind in life. Help me remember the empty tomb.

Discussion:

1. Describe the most amazing come-back game you have ever played in or seen.

2. What difference does it make in your experience that Jesus was raised from the dead?

Passion

Football Friday! I couldn't wait until 7:00 p.m. Kickoff time! The first game of the year! I was pumped throughout the day!

Just as much as I look forward to Friday night football, King David longed to be in God's presence. He couldn't wait. It was his one focus, just to be in the presence of the living God.

"My soul yearns, even faints, for the courts of the Lord; my heart and my flesh cry out for the living God." (Psalm 84:2)

You don't have to go to church to cry out. Your kitchen table will do just fine, or that worn-out couch in your coaches' office.

Lord, give me a heart for You, just like David. Let me have the same passion about being in Your presence that I have for Friday night football. Amen

Discussion:

1. Describe the most enthusiastic fan you have ever seen at a game.

2. Read Psalm 42. How does David feel about meeting with God?

3. Ask God to give you a desire to be with Him.

Potential

What do you see in that seventh-grader who has a difficult time just dribbling the ball up the court? Does he look like a future point guard? What do we see in the freshman pitcher who most days throws more balls than strikes?

Jesus always saw potential in people. He sees it in us. He sees it in us even when our behavior suggests otherwise.

Look at Jesus' first interaction with the disciple who would later be one of His key guys.

"The first thing Andrew did was to find his brother Simon and tell him, 'We have found the Messiah' (that is, the Christ). And Andrew brought him to Jesus. Jesus looked at him and said, 'You are Simon son of John, You will be called 'Cephas' (which translated is Peter.'") (John 1:41-42)

The name Peter means rock.

When Peter first meets Jesus, Peter is not a rock. Jesus knew it would take a long time for Simon to become that rock, but He hung in there with Peter, the same way He hangs in there with us. He never lost sight of the potential in Peter.

Lord, thanks for looking at me to see my potential by Your grace. Help me look at others the same way, through the eyes of grace. I want my Jesus glasses on so I can see the way You do.

Discussion:

1. Can you recall someone you coached who didn't look like much to begin with but came on later to become a great player?

2. What are some things Peter did that demonstrated he was not a rock? What happens to Peter to make him that rock?

3. Do you feel more like a rock or marshmallow?

Take off the White Hat

The guy in the white hat and black and white striped shirt blew the whistle. "Five-yard penalty. Offsides. Offense."

Who is this guy in the white hat and striped shirt? He is the head referee. He makes all the calls as he sees them. He is the final authority on the field of play.

"There is only one Lawgiver and one Judge, the one who is able to save and destroy. But you—who are you to judge your neighbor?" (James 4:12)

In the game of life, I love to wear that white hat. You know, blow the whistle and make all the calls. Make judgments about situations and people. Penalize others for not doing it the way I would do it or looking the way I would look. But I always mess up. I hurt myself, and I hurt other people when I don't let God be God and leave the calls to Him.

Lord, keep me from judging others and let me leave those calls to You. Just keep me loving people, not judging them. Help me to feed the sheep, not eat the sheep. I take off the whistle and give it to You.

Discussion:

1. Describe some situations in which you often find yourself judging or criticizing others.

2. Why is a referee in a better position to make a call than a spectator in the stands?

3. What is one thing you can do to stop judging and letting God do that?

Finish Strong

Two runners battled each other for 1598 meters. Back and forth. Back and forth. One took the lead, then the other. The winner of the 1600 meter run wasn't decided until the final two meters.

The most exciting part of any game, and indeed any race, is the finish. Lots of games are won or lost in the final seconds. Many a race is won or lost in the last few yards.

Jesus was a finisher. He was a completer. He got to the finish line. He made it to the cross and on the way trained a group of guys to carry on His work when he left.

"My food," said Jesus, is to do the will of Him who sent me and to finish His work.'" (John 4:34)

Jesus was all about finishing His Father's work. What are some things that keep us from completing life's tasks? Perhaps we get distracted. Maybe we lose hope. Maybe we just lose sight of the value of finishing.

So if it is a daily task like grading a set of papers or planning a practice schedule, ask God to help you finish well. If it is a lifelong goal, ask God to help you finish.

Lord, help me finish well today on the field and in my life. Keep me going. Keep me showing up. Help me get to the finish line and run the race well.

Discussion:

1. Share the last time you were distracted and did not finish something.

2. What is something that you need to finish soon?

3. How could God help you be a better finisher?

Reconditioned

It happens every year. Football coaches send away their equipment to be reconditioned. It is packed up, shipped off and comes back looking like new.

"Because of the Lord's great love we are not consumed, for His compassions never fail. They are NEW every morning; great is Your faithfulness." (Lamentations 3:22-23)

God is in the business of making everything new. Perhaps the piece of equipment that most needs reconditioning is our hearts. Hearts hurt by the blows of the world, hearts cracked by head-on collisions with the forces of life, hairline cracks in our souls from misunderstanding or unforgiveness.

We all need restoring. It is a difficult thing to admit we need some reconditioning, but God is more than willing to take the old, the cracked and the overused and send it back new.

Lord, I am sending my heart to You. It needs repair. It needs to be made new. In Jesus' name. Amen.

Discussion:

1. What is an area of your life you would like to see reconditioned?

2. What is a relationship you would like to see God make new?

Name Calling

Champ. That was our son Matt's nickname growing up. Instead of calling him Matt all the time, sometimes I would just call him Champ.

The names we call other people make an impact. Sometimes those names become our identity.

The disciple John never got over the fact that Jesus loved him. When he wrote the book of John and referred to himself, he often just called himself "the disciple whom Jesus loved."

You are the coach Jesus loves. Right there at your desk, and on the field and in your home. He will always love you. Let that be your identity wherever your feet touch the ground: concrete, grass, turf, wood or the rug at home.

"For I am convinced that neither death nor life, neither angels nor demons, neither the present nor the future, nor any powers, neither height nor depth, nor anything else in all creation, will be able to separate us from the love of God that is in Christ Jesus our Lord." (Romans 8:38)

You are loved. 10-0. 0-10.

Lord, thank You for loving me and that no behavior of mine will ever pull the plug on that love. May my being loved by You be my greatest claim to fame.

Discussion:

1. Share some both positive and negative nicknames you remember others calling you or others.

2. Do you see yourself more as a coach who is a Christian or a Christian who is a coach?

3. What some positive names you can begin to use to address some of the players on your team today?

Spread Offense

The spread offense is a formation where receivers line up from sideline to sideline to spread out the defense.

Many football teams employ the spread offense for various reasons. I think of another spread offense. This one was a person whose arms spread wide, not the width of a field, but the width of a cross. Jesus' arms nailed to a cross, spread for you and me. It was the ultimate offense, designed not to cross a goal line but to take on the sin of the world.

"The reason the Son of God appeared was to destroy the works of the devil." (1 John 3:8)

The next time you are at a football game and see the offense spread from sideline to sideline, think of the One who spread his arms wide so you and I could watch that game.

Lord, thanks for going to the cross for me, for surrendering. I am grateful.

Discussion:

1. What are some advantages of running the spread offense?

2. What impact does it have on you to know Jesus died on a cross rather than just dying from something like a heart attack?

Smelling Good!

Cramergesic is one of my all-time favorite athletic smells. Just a whiff evokes memories of track meets and competition on warm spring afternoons.

Former girls' track coach at Bellevue High School, the late Pep Stidham, used to keep a tub of Cramergesic in the trunk of his car during track season. One summer after track season he forgot it and left it in there. The Cramergesic melted into the carpet of his trunk, and the smell wafted throughout the entire car! Opening up the car was like opening up a tub of that red gel.

The Bible tells us that we, too, have a smell about us as Christians. The smell of Christ.

"But thanks be to God, who always leads us in triumphal procession in Christ and through us spreads everywhere the fragrance of the knowledge of him." (2 Corinthians 2:14)

May the Lord take the lid off our lives and fill our homes, classrooms and athletic fields with the fragrance of Jesus.

Lord, help me smell up my school and my home with the fragrance of Christ. Fill me with Your Spirit and take the lid off the bottle! May my house and fields be as smelly of Jesus as the locker room is of sweat and dirty socks!

Discussion:

1. What is a favorite scent you associate with athletics?

2. If the fragrance of Christ could be measured in your life, on a scale of 1-10 how much do you give off that aroma?

3. What are some things you could do to make your fragrance a little stronger?

Time Out

The whistle blows, and both teams head for the sidelines. The referee turns toward the goal line and motions with his hands. "Timeout, white."

Timeouts are a good thing. They give the coach a chance to talk face-to-face with his team and get closer than yelling from the sidelines. Every player knows that when a timeout is called, they need to head for the sidelines.

Jesus extends to us the same timeout offer.

"Come to Me, all you who are weary and burdened, and I will give you rest. Take my yoke upon you and learn from Me, for I am gentle and humble in heart, and you will find rest for your souls. For my yoke is easy and my burden is light." (Matthew 11:28)

Weary? Burdened? Whatever you are experiencing on the field of life, take a timeout, go to the sidelines and just talk to Jesus. He just might have a good idea on that third and long situation you are facing. Don't stay on the field. Go to the sidelines and listen.

Lord, I am tired. It has been a long day and a long season. I come to You weary and burdened. Rest my soul.

Discussion:

1. Share a time when a timeout impacted the outcome of a game or match.

2. Do you have a regular timeout in your day? If so when is it? Tell us about it.

3. If you do not have a regular timeout scheduled, when would be a good time to have that?

Breakfast for Champions

Just after his resurrection, Jesus met his disciples on the Sea of Galilee. The last time Jesus had seen them, they were hightailing it away from the mob that arrested Jesus. Now days later, the disciples, disappointed and discouraged, had fished all night and caught nothing. On the shore, Jesus yelled to the disciples, "Cast your net on the right side of the boat!" At His direction, the disciples cast their net on the other side and caught 153 trophy fish.

When they arrived on shore, Jesus told the disciples, "Come and have breakfast." (John 21:12)

A very generous invitation, especially in light of their abandonment of Jesus only days before. No lecture. No condemnation. Just some mighty tasty fish!

One of the most difficult times in a coach's life is responding well when an athlete performs poorly. I wish I could say I had been as gracious as Jesus, but I have chewed out my share of athletes, including my own son.

Jesus' invitation, on the other hand, is pure mercy. They don't get what they deserve (a lecture). Instead, they get what they don't deserve (a meal).

Lord, make me a merciful coach. Help me give my athletes a breakfast of encouragement when they need it most, when they have failed. May I be as merciful toward them as You are toward me.

Discussion:

1. Share a fishing story of yours with the group.

2. Share a difficult time in your life when someone encouraged you. What impact did that have on you?

Receivers

Jerry Rice. A.J. Green. Raymond Barry. All great receivers. It was their job to run the route, catch the ball and get more yardage if they could.

God's Kingdom is full of receivers. Not earners. Receivers. God's Kingdom belongs to people who have put their hands out and received God's love and forgiveness in Jesus. It is a gift, not a spiritual paycheck for doing good deeds or avoiding the Nasty Nine or the Dirty Dozen.

"But to as many as received Him, to them (the receivers) God gave the right to become His children, even to those who believe on His name." (John 1:12)

Try this. Right now at your computer or if you are holding your smart phone, just put out your hands. No one will suspect. Tell God you want to receive Him and all He has for you today.

Lord, there is just something inside me that makes me feel like I have to earn what I get. Earn favor, earn salvation, earn forgiveness. Jesus, help me realize I can just receive. I open my hands and my heart to You.

Discussion:

1. Who is the best receiver you have ever coached or seen play on another team?

2. Do you see yourself trying to earn God's love?

3. What makes it hard for men to be receivers?

Be a Fullback

The job description for a fullback is short - block. Not a lot of players sign up for that. There's not a lot of opportunity to carry the ball, just the chance to clear the way for the running back and let him pick up the yards while the fullback and linebackers meet head-on near the line of scrimmage.

John the Baptist would have made a great fullback. His job description was also short—block for Jesus. Prepare the way for Jesus.

"As it is written in Isaiah the prophet: I will send my messenger ahead of you, who will prepare your way—a voice of one crying in the desert, 'Prepare the way of the Lord, make straight paths for him.' " (Mark 1:2-3)

John the Baptist was the messenger. It was his job to prepare the way so that when Jesus showed up, people were ready.

God is still looking for good fullbacks, people who are willing to prepare the way for others.

For whom could you be the fullback today? Your spouse? A fellow teacher or coach? A player? What could you do to make their way straight, to get some of the obstacles facing them out of the way?

Lord, I would much rather carry the ball if You don't mind, even hand it off. But block for someone? That's just not me. Obviously, I need some help in this area. Allow me to see people at school or my team or in my home for whom I could help clear the way. Help me be a good fullback in my heart.

Discussion:

1. Who are some great fullbacks you recall from your teams or others?

2. Describe some character traits that make a good fullback.

3. Look at the questions above in the final paragraph and answer them.

Lost

Coach, ever feel lost? Lost in too much pressure? Lost in too many relational problems on the team? Lost trying to keep your team, your administration and your marriage afloat during the season?

One of the parables Jesus teaches is about a lost sheep, one of 100. When the one sheep gets lost, the shepherd leaves the 99 and searches for the one until he finds it. When he does locate the sheep, the Bible says, the shepherd "joyfully puts it on his shoulders and goes home."(Luke 15:5)

The Bible doesn't say that this was a real prize sheep. It could have been one of the scruffy ones: wool matted, hooves cut from rocks, and one horn missing. "No one is even going to miss me," that sheep might have thought.

There are times we all feel like scruffy sheep. Irritated from too many meetings. Exhausted from long, hot summer practices, and now the season is not going well.

God wants you to know that you are worth looking for, and when He finds you, you make Him happy.

Lord, I do get lost so often. Thank You for always finding me. I get so easily distracted, and honestly, there are times I just sneak off hoping You won't notice. Thanks for coming to look for me and being happy when You find me. That's incredible!

Discussion:

1. Tell about a time you got lost while traveling. How did you figure out the correct direction?

2. Have you ever felt lost emotionally? Just didn't know where to go? Tell us about it.

3. Did someone come looking for you and find you when you were lost?

Friday Night Lights

Ever been to a Friday night football game in the country? Everything may be dark around the field, but the 100 X 52-yard grass area is as bright as the noonday sun on a summer day.

A small band of shepherds outside Bethlehem must have felt like they had just walked onto a football field in the country. All was dark around them, but suddenly the sky was filled with light as "the glory of the Lord shone around them . . ." (Luke 2:9)

Jesus was born not just that the shepherds' sky would be brighter but that our hearts would be more hopeful as well. Light for them in the heavens. Light for us in our hearts.

Jesus came "to shine on those living darkness . . ." (Luke 1:79) He came to be the "field light" of your soul. All we have to do is receive that light.

Like a flip of the switch lights a darkened football field, a decision of our hearts toward Jesus turns on the light in our soul.

The next time you watch a football game at night, may the brightness of the field remind you that a small child was born to be the light of the world and to fill your heart with light.

Lord, life does feel like playing in the dark sometimes. It's hard to see where I am going, and I run into others a lot. Would You be my light? Turn on the switch of Your presence and light up my world.

Discussion:

1. Ever play a game in the country? What are some unusual elements of that setting?

2. What is the brightest light you have ever seen?

3. Right now, what is a dark place in your life where you could use a little of God's light?

Regret

An ESPN sideline analyst overheard the Auburn head football coach say after their quarterback threw an incomplete pass, "He should've run the ball!"

Regrets. Missed opportunities. As coaches, we face regrets after almost every game: dropped passes, missed shots, and wrong plays called.

God has a way of taking our shoulds, our regrets, and making them all a part of His plan. He is able to take our incomplete passes and turn them into touchdowns.

"And we know that God causes all things to work together for good to those who love God and are called according to His purpose." (Romans 8:28)

God has a purpose, and He is working it out in each of our lives. When we drop the ball, instead of being overwhelmed with regret, invite God into the mix and let Him work it out for good, according to His game plan.

Lord, I have a locker room full of regrets. Things I said to my son I wish had not been said. Game decisions that could have been better. Living for the moment rather than for the long haul. I give all those regrets to You. Would You take them and make something good from them? Thank you for having a purpose for me.

Discussion:

1. If you could do instant replay on any one call or moment in your life, what would it be and why?

2. Why do coaches have such a tendency to focus on the negatives of any athletic contest?

3. Share a personal regret you have?

The Player Coach

One of the great advantages of having played the sport you coach is that you can identify with your players. Been there. Done that. Shot 100 free throws. Ran suicides until you puked. It also helps your players know you once did what you are asking them to do.

In the same way, Jesus can identify with us. There is no event, no emotion, no circumstance that Jesus has not experienced. When we pray, we can be assured Jesus understands.

"For we do not have a high priest who cannot sympathize with our weaknesses, but One who in all ways has been tempted as we are yet without sin. Let us, therefore, approach the throne of grace with confidence that we may receive mercy and grace to help in time of need." (Hebrews 4: 15-16)

Jesus felt the pain of disappointment, the tug of lust, the loneliness of rejection. When you knock on His door, there will be no lecture, just mercy and grace. Don't worry about wearing out your welcome. He will always be happy you came to see Him.

Lord, thank you that You understand. Thank you for understanding my weaknesses and that I can come to You on a moment's notice. Thanks for putting on skin and being made like a man. That makes me want to come to You more often.

Discussion:

1. Can you recall an incident in which you told a player about a workout you did or something that happened to you as an athlete to help the athlete know what you had been through and that you could identify with them?

2. How does it make you feel knowing Jesus can identify with the events of your life?

3. What are some negative emotions Jesus experienced that are similar to those a coach could experience?

Knock, Knock!

A knock comes at the door of your office. You are busy putting the finishing touches on the day's practice schedule. "Come in!" you yell, and an anxious seventh grader enters, telling you he needs to talk.

Jesus says in Revelation 3:20 "Behold I stand at the door and knock. If anyone hears my voice and opens the door, I will come into him and will fellowship with him and he with Me."

Great invitation. Marvelous opportunity. Not just once but for every day of our lives.

The next time someone knocks on your classroom door or the coaches' office door, let it remind you of God's desire to get into the mix of your life and make a difference for you. Open the door. Ask Him to come in.

Lord, I open the door of my life and invite You in, not just as a guest but as someone who will stay for the long haul. Thank you for coming in and coming in to stay.

Discussion:

1. Share a time when you knocked on a coach's office door and how you felt.

2. Why is it hard for athletes to knock on a coach's office door?

3. If Jesus said He would come into your life and hang out with you, what do you imagine the two of you doing?

4. What does Jesus' invitation suggest about how He views you?

Pressure

The full-court press. Sometimes it's hard just to get the ball in-bounds, much less across mid-court. A well-conditioned pressing team can dismantle a more talented team in a matter of minutes. The result? Bad passes, turnovers and frustration for the pressed team, and easy scores for the pressing team.

Life can feel like we are on the receiving end of the full-court press, and life is doing everything it can to keep us from just getting the ball across mid-court, much less score. We feel the press of expectations, hectic scheduling and disrupted relationships.

A guy named Paul experienced the press of life.

"We do not want you to be uninformed, brothers, about the hardships we suffered in the province of Asia. We were under great pressure, far beyond our ability to endure, so that we despaired even of life...But this happened that we might not rely on ourselves but on God, who raises the dead." (2 Corinthians 1:8-9)

Sometimes pressures in life, like dealing with the full-court press, make us realize we have to make adjustments. For Paul, the adjustment was that he could no longer rely on his abilities; he had to rely on God.

Lord, was the guy who wrote that verse a coach? Pressure? Yes! Even if there wasn't a booster club or angry parents, I put so much pressure on myself. I feel like I am a perfectionist in every area of my life. So I come to You. I am going to start relying more on You and less on me. I think that might work a little better.

Discussion:

1. Share a time the opposing team effectively executed a press against your team.

2. Share an area of your life in which you feel pressure right now.

Pin!

The wrestler shot in with a double-leg takedown! Before his opponent knew it, he was on his back. PIN!

Sometimes the hardest things for us to take down are not physical opponents but our thoughts. Sometimes those thoughts run wild, like a class of kindergarten kids after lunch. Thoughts like bitterness, anger, resentment, and lust run around in our brains, demanding more and more of our attention.

God's Word paints a vivid word picture of what we are to do with those unwanted mental trespassers.

"For though we live in this world, we do not wage war as the world does. The weapons we fight with are not the weapons of the world...we take captive every thought to make it obedient to Christ." (2 Corinthians 10:3-5)

Perhaps it is time to put on our wrestling singlets and pin those thoughts to the mat. The sooner we take them down, the less time we have to wrestle with them.

Lord, so many thoughts swirling in my mind. Help me pin them to the ground, never to get up again. Let's take care of those imaginations in the first period and not wait until the end of the match.

Discussion:

1. What is the quickest pin you have ever witnessed in a wrestling match?

2. What are some thoughts with which you are currently wrestling?

Disappointment

If you have been coaching for any length of time, you have likely experienced disappointment. Not many other activities have the potential of swinging us so wildly between the mountaintops or the valleys of life.

After Jesus' death, a couple of guys were walking along a country road to a place called Emmaus. Jesus walked up to them, but they didn't recognize Him. The story says "their faces were downcast." Disappointed. When asked why they were disappointed they said, "...we had hoped that He was the one who was going to redeem Israel." Jesus didn't meet their expectations, and they were disappointed.

What encouragement is there in our disappointments? I read a verse this morning after I had eaten my oatmeal and raisins, "...and the one who trusts in Me will never be disappointed." (Romans 9:33)

Yes, we will all be disappointed by life's circumstances: a late-season loss, an injury to a key player, not achieving a team goal, but Jesus never disappoints.

It is okay to be disappointed. That's part of coaching. As soon as you can though, invite Jesus into the mix and ask Him to make a difference.

Lord, I get disappointed so much. I tend to focus on the negative and not on all the good things that happen. Help me shift my expectations to You.

Discussion:

1. Share a time when you were disappointed as a coach.

2. What difference would it make in our attitude if we went into an athletic event trusting in Jesus, rather than trusting in the performance of a 16-17-year-old?

The One Guy

In basketball, the point guard is the 'one.' The position carries much responsibility: bring the ball up the floor, direct the flow of the offense, and reset the offense if a play doesn't work. He must be able to see the entire floor and anticipate the movement of the defense. Key guy.

Jesus wants to have that position in our lives. He can see the full court and control our lives better than we can ourselves. Just like the point guard on the basketball floor, He has to have the ball. For Him to function in the 'one' position in our lives, though, we have to give Him control.

"And He is the head of the body, the church; He is the beginning and the firstborn from among the dead so that He might come to have first place in everything." (Colossians 1:18)

Who guides the offense of your life now? Giving Jesus the ball is as easy as saying, "Here, Lord, I give myself and the stuff of my life to You."

As you watch the next basketball game and you see the point guard bringing the ball up the floor, remind yourself of Jesus' desire to be that 'one' guy for you. Enjoy the game!

Lord, I feel I spend a lot of time asking people to pass me the ball. "I'm open! I'm open!" I spend a lot of time in the 'one' position of my heart. I think I will give You the ball and let You call the offense of my life. There are four other guys on the team. Maybe one of them is open!

Discussion:

1. Who are some of the best point guards you have seen play? What made them so effective?

2. Can you recall any ball hogs you have seen play?

Finishing

Starting is easy. Continuing is hard. The first set is easier; the second set is more difficult. The first 200 is easier; the second 200 is harder. The third 200 is harder still!

God wants us to be good finishers, not just good starters.

"And now, dear children, continue in Him, so that when he appears we may be confident and unashamed at His coming." (1 John 2:28)

Where is a place you would like God's help continuing? In the class-room, grading that final set of papers? On the field, finishing the practice strong and positive? At home, being entirely focused on your mate and children? In your marriage of 30 years, not being dis-tracted by comparing a 16-year-old to a 56-year-old?

The key? Continuing in Him. We can't do this alone. We need God to get to the finish line.

God, help us continue in You. Keep on doing the next right thing. Keep on taking the next right step. Help me get to the finish line glad that I continued in You.

Discussion:

1. What is hardest about the final quarter or last set or final mile?

2. What do you think of when you think of the word "continue"?

3. Share an area of your life in which you feel you are "fading" rather than "continuing." Pray now and ask God to help you make it to the finish.

Locker Room Resurrection

Imagine your team uniform lying on the floor in your locker room. The jersey in its place and the pants in their place, but no one is wearing the jersey. No one is wearing the pants. They are just lying there in the same form as if someone were wearing them.

That's what the disciples saw when they looked inside the tomb. "Then Simon Peter, who was behind him, arrived and went into the tomb. He saw the strips of linen lying there..." (John 20:6)

The strips of cloth that had wrapped around Jesus were just lying there in the shape of a person. No one had taken them off. They were not wadded up. Just lying there, collapsed.

Next time you see one of your athlete's uniforms just lying around, let it remind you of Jesus who "came out of an empty tomb to fill our empty hearts."

Lord, thank You for the resurrection. Help me to live more fully in the truth that You are alive.

Discussion:

1. Take a roll of pre-wrap and unroll it to form the shape of a body lying on the floor. That's how Jesus' empty grave clothes looked. What if the strips of linen had not been there. What might have been some of the possible explanations?

3. Why was it important that the pieces of cloth were still there?

We Need Each Other

The right guard said to the right tackle, "I don't need you!"

A member of the tennis doubles team said to his partner, "I don't need you!"

The head coach said to one of his assistants, "I don't need you!"

The husband said to his wife, "I don't need you!"

"Now the body is not made up of one part but of many...in fact, God has arranged the parts in the body, every one of them, just as he wanted them to be. If they were all one part, where would the body be? As it is, there are many parts, but one body...Now you are the body of Christ, and each one of you is a part of it." (1 Corinthians 12:14, 18-19, 27)

The right guard **does** need the right tackle. Do you want to block this guy by yourself?

The doubles team tennis player **does** need his partner. Do you want to cover the entire court by yourself?

The head coach **does** need his assistant. Do you want to coach every position by yourself?

The husband **does** need his wife. Do you want to come home to an empty house today?

Lord, I struggle so much with being independent and thinking I don't need anyone else. You call that pride. Help me see how much I truly need other people and give them a chance to help me.

Discussion:

1. Why do we feel we don't need each other?

2. Think of someone you need. Now call that person or write them a note and tell them how important they are to you

A Prayer

Coaches, rather than write something for you, I would simply like to pray for you.

God, I thank you for these coaches. I pray you would encourage them. I pray they would know how much You love them. Would You encourage those whose teams have been ravaged by injuries? Would You support the coach who lost a close game last Friday night? Would You comfort the coach who hasn't had a lot of time at home in a few weeks? Would You help the coach to repair strained relationships with his players? Would You help us to see the heart under the jersey?

Lord, You said in Your Word, "Never will I leave you; never will I forsake you. So we may say with confidence, 'The Lord is my helper; I will not be afraid. What can man do to me?'" (Hebrews 13:5) May Your promise to never leave us be an encouragement to each of these coaches.

Lord, You said in Your Word, "In You, all things hold together." (Colossians 1:17) Would you hold these coaches together emotionally, spiritually and physically? Would You keep their teams together? Would You keep their marriages together?

May You do it all for their sakes and Yours. Amen.

Discussion:

1. Do you ever pray for your colleagues? Your athletes?

2. How might taking time regularly to pray for them impact your coaching?

Hold Up

One of the saddest pictures in the athletic world is witnessing an injury to an athlete that requires the assistance of several people just to get the athlete off the field or court.

I read the following verse as I waited for the girls to get back from a run this morning. The last part of Hebrews 1:3 says that Jesus "...upholds all things by the word of His power."

Sometimes we just need Jesus to hold us up, to get under each arm and get us to the sideline. When we read God's Word, it is like Jesus holding us up. God's Word has the power to hold us up.

I encourage you to read some verses that talk about Jesus and who He is. Hebrews 1:1-4, Colossians 1:15-20, and John 1:1-18 are good "hold you up" truth. (You can go to Bible Gateway on your computer.)

Lord, I pray You would hold up these coaches today, by the Word of Your Power. Hold them up in the classroom, on the practice field and court and in their homes.

Discussion:

1. Have you ever been injured and needed someone to help you walk?

2. In what areas do you feel Jesus needs to hold you up?

3. Who could use you to hold them up? Make an effort to connect with that person today.

The Call

Imagine the referee making the following call after one play. "Offsides, personal foul, holding, chop block, unsportsmanlike conduct, pass interference, number 23, offense." I'll bet number 23 would be looking for a good place to hide! All those penalties on just one person!!

Genuinely, on another field far away in Jerusalem, over 2000 years ago Jesus Christ took on himself all the penalties of humankind in a single play. It was called The Cross.

"He (God) made Him (Jesus) who knew no sin, to be sin on our behalf, that we might become the righteousness of God in Him." (2 Corinthians 5:21)

All my lying, meanness, self-centeredness, pretending, insecurity, lust, shame, exaggerating and not just mine but all the penalties of the whole world, Jesus took on Himself, willingly, so you and I could have a chance to connect to His Father eternally.

At the next football game, listen when the referee calls a penalty. Thank God that Jesus took all of your penalties on the cross.

Thank you, Lord, for not just arranging to pay for my sin but for actually paying for it Yourself, for actually becoming my sin. I accept Your payment and receive forgiveness and rightness before You. That's a great deal!

Discussion:

1. Read the list of penalties in Ephesians 5:19-21. Which is most glaring in your life?

2. Now say "Because of Jesus' death on the cross, you are forgiven" to each person in the group.

Encroachment

A player from the defensive team crosses over into the neutral zone before the ball snaps. Only a five-yard penalty, but it can keep a drive alive for the offense. Sometimes little things are very costly.

God's Word talks about three things that can be encroachments in our lives: worry, lust and greed.

"Still other people are like seed sown among thorns. They hear the word, but the worries of the world, the deceitfulness of riches, and the desires for other things enter in and choke the word, making it unfruitful." (Mark 4:18-19)

When I was coaching, I had to contend with these three thorns on a regular basis. I would be wary of the accolades that accompanied winning a game or a meet that had the potential to draw me away from God.

The desire for success often choked out my heart for God. I wanted success more than I wanted God.

If these thorns plague your life as well, join me as I pray for us.

Lord, some days it seems my life is one big thorn patch. My worries and my wants rush into the offense of my life and kill any desire I have to pray or read Your Word. Help me, Lord. Would You tend the garden of my life and help me get rid of these thorns?

Discussion:

1. Which of the three thorns most plagues your life: worries of the world, the deceitfulness of riches or the desires for other things?

2. What can you do to loosen the choking grip of these issues in your life?

Hope

The scoreboard clock read "0:00." Game over. "Put 4 seconds back on the clock," the referee barked over his microphone.

A guy by the name of Jairus also needed more time on the clock. He had just asked Jesus to come and heal his daughter, but on the way to his home, some messengers arrived informing Jairus that his daughter had died. Game over.

"Ignoring what they said (that the daughter was indeed dead), Jesus told the synagogue ruler (Jairus), "Don't be afraid; just believe." (Mark 5:36)

The presence of Jesus puts more time on our clock. When all is lost and life offers us despair, the presence of Jesus can give us hope.

Jesus arrived at Jairus' house and found the report was accurate. Jairus' daughter was indeed dead.

Jesus entered the room where the child was. "And taking the child by the hand, He said to her, 'Little girl, I say to you arise' And immediately the girl got up and began to walk; for she was twelve years old." (Mark 5:41-42)

Jesus, give me hope today. Put hope back on the clock of my life, hope for my team, for my family, for myself.

Discussion:

1. Can you recall a time when the referee put more time on the clock and it affected the outcome of the game?

2. Share a situation where you would like to see Jesus put more time on the clock.

3. Who do you know facing a situation like Jairus? They might need a little encouragement from you today.

Alone

Coaching can be a very lonely experience. Even though we have assistant coaches and even a supportive community around us, we can feel very alone.

A verse in Mark recently caught my attention. Jesus had just finished feeding 5,000 people using five loaves and two fish. He sent the disciples away in their boat, sent the crowd away and went up on a mountainside to pray.

"When evening came, the boat was in the middle of the lake, and He was alone on the land." (Mark 6:47)

I never think of Jesus being alone, but it helps me to know He understands when I am alone. Sometimes I feel alone after a game. The stands are empty. The team is gone. The excitement is over, and I am alone.

Jesus is speaking in John 8:29, "The one who sent Me is with Me; He has not left Me alone, for I always do what pleases Him."

"Be strong and courageous. Do not be afraid or terrified because of them (your enemies) for the Lord your God goes with you; He will never leave you or forsake you." (Deuteronomy 31:6)

Lord, thank You for the assurance of Your presence. When I feel alone, even in a crowd, may I remember that You will never leave me or forsake me.

Discussion:

1. Recall a time when you felt especially lonely.

2. How has God met you in those alone times?

3. What was Jesus doing when He was alone? Do you have an intentional alone time with Jesus every day? When could that time be if you do not?

Plus Yardage

Would you rather run a play for negative five yards or positive ten yards? Would you rather be behind by four at the half or ahead by eight?

Isaiah 61:7 says, "Instead of their shame my people will receive a double portion, and instead of disgrace they will rejoice in their inheritance, and so they will inherit a double portion in their land, and everlasting joy will be theirs."

God wants to give you a double portion, kind of like +20 yards rather than just +10. However, sometimes shame puts us in the minus column, like negative ten yards rather than negative five.

The definition of shame is 'failure of being.' The definition of blame is 'failure of doing.' Shame puts us in the minus yardage of life: shame over the past, shame regarding an addiction or habit, shame over a broken relationship.

Jesus took your shame on the cross. God wants to take your guilt and replace it with His joy. He took all of the plays for lost yardage of our lives and died for that on the cross.

If you feel shame today, give Him all the minus yardage incidents of your life.

Lord, I do feel shame for things I have done, but the worst is I just feel shame for who I am. I need You to tell me who I am and not allow the other influences on my life to define me. May Your voice be the loudest voice.

Discussion:

1. How might a team feel if they had a minus-yardage total for an entire game?

2. How does a play end in minus yardage?

3. Share a play for minus yardage you have experienced in your life recently.

A Handful

Billy Bob was a great athlete at Boonesville High, a tremendous football player and track athlete. As the expression goes though, he was a handful. You just never know what Billy Bob might have up his sleeve. Perhaps you have had athletes on your team like Billy Bob. You had to keep your eye on them.

God may feel that way about us at times. Maybe we are a handful to him. There was another guy in the Bible who was hard to manage. His name was Ephraim. Here's what God says about him.

"Is not Ephraim my dear son, the child in whom I delight? Though I often speak against him, I still remember him. Therefore my heart yearns for him; I have great compassion for him,' declares the Lord." (Jeremiah 31:20)

Wow! Even though Ephraim has been a handful to God, even though God spoke against him, God still has great compassion for him.

God feels the same about you. Maybe today you feel like you have given God a hard time. But God still remembers you. His heart yearns for you. He calls you His dear child, and He delights in you.

Lord, I have given You a hard time. I have not cooperated with You. I have been rebellious and self-centered. Thank You for delighting in me in spite of how I have treated You and others. It is hard to believe that I make You happy, but I'll take it that I do!

Discussion:

1. Recall an athlete of yours who was a handful. Were you able to delight in him or her?

2. What is something you do that gives you pleasure?

3. Do you feel like you are a joy to God? He says you are! Pray now and thank God that He takes great delight in you.

Super Winners

The Super Bowl is not just any old game. It is not the Honey Nut Cheerios Bowl or the Tidy Bowl. It is THE game of the year!

In Romans chapter 8, Paul lists a set of life's difficulties. These challenges include "trouble and hardship (maybe losing the game on a last-second shot), persecution (from a disgruntled parent), or famine (no wins yet), or nakedness (worn uniforms) or danger (tough crowd in the stands) or sword (heard gunshots last night as we left the gym)." (Romans 8:35)

However, the Bible says that people who may experience these things are more than regular winners, they are super winners just because God loves them. God's love helps us win even when we experience the adverse situations listed above. Just knowing that none of those circumstances will ever stop God from loving you is a difference maker.

"No, in all these things we are more than conquerors through Him who loved us." (Romans 8:37)

Lord, most of the times I feel conquered rather than a conqueror. Take me to the "more than" level. I'm not sure what that means, but I would like to go there with You.

Discussion:

1. Recall a situation you have been in where you felt you were in danger. How did you respond?

2. Have you experienced any of the situations listed in the second paragraph?

3. The fact that God loves you gives super conqueror status. Pray now and thank God that because of His love you are a super conqueror!

Underinflated or Overinflated?

Underinflated or overinflated? Both scenarios can give us trouble.

The game ball of life is hard to grip when we overinflate ourselves. Coaching can do that. It puts extra air into our heads, and our attempts to connect with other people fall short or just don't happen.

God says in Philippians chapter 2, verse 3, "Do nothing out of selfish ambition or vain conceit, but in humility consider others better than yourselves."

The cure for an overinflated life? Let some of the air of self out.

Underinflation can also be a problem. Sometimes we don't have enough power or energy to get through practice, classes, and being a good dad, mom, husband, or wife. The Bible says in Ephesians 5:18, "Do not get drunk with wine, which leads to debauchery. Instead, be filled with the Spirit."

The cure for an underinflated life? Be filled with God's Spirit. Let God's Spirit control your life, not outside influences.

Lord, put just the right amount of inflation in my life. Keep me from thinking too highly of myself. Stop me from thinking too little of myself. How about I think more of You and others.

Discussion:

1. Recall a time you felt your life was overinflated. Share that with the group.

2. Remember a time you felt your life was underinflated. Share that with the group.

3. What does Jesus do in Philippians 2 to deal with overinflation?

4. Romans 12 tells us to "outdo one another in giving honor." Think of someone you can honor this week. Honor means to give high value to something or someone.

Encouragement from the Chairs

Two weeks ago my wife and I attended the regional wrestling tournament at a local high school. During each match I noticed every wrestler had two coaches sitting in chairs in the corner of his mat, encouraging him and giving him direction. The coach was fully engaged with his team's wrestler, watching every move.

The Bible tells us we have our cheering section with more than just people in two chairs, rather a crowd of individuals there to encourage us and give us direction.

Hebrews 12:1,2 says, "Since we are surrounded by such a great cloud of witnesses, let us run with endurance the race that is set before us. Fixing our eyes on Jesus, who for the joy set before Him endured the cross and has sat down at the right hand of the majesty on high."

You are surrounded! So many people are cheering for you. Read Hebrews chapter 11 for a list of those seated in the stands! You may feel like you are about to be pinned or are running out of strength in the final period, but look over at the chairs. God and many others are there, cheering for you! Hear their voices of encouragement today!

Lord, that's quite an audience cheering for me! Help me listen to their applause and cheering when my endurance is running low.

Discussion:

1. Have you ever been to a wrestling match? What were the coaches in the chairs doing?

2. Who is someone who has been in the chairs of your life, cheering for you?

3. Think of someone for whom you could sit in the chairs and encourage today?

Thirsty

We all have our go-to drink when we are physically thirsty. However, when we are emotionally or spiritually thirsty, we again have our different drinks. We go to different wells. Sometimes we drink from the well of athletic success, at times from the latest victory, or from an award we have received or from the remarks of someone we admire. There's nothing wrong with those wells, but they just won't satisfy for the long haul. We need another, more satisfying drink after a while.

Jesus spoke to a woman at a well once who was drinking from the well of having been married five times, and even then she was living with yet another man. She was not satisfied.

Jesus told the woman, "Everyone who drinks this water (success, reputation, honor) will get thirsty again. But whoever drinks the water I give him will never thirst. Indeed, the water I give him will become in him a spring of water welling up to eternal life." (John 4:13-14)

The best well is the Jesus well.

Lord, I find myself thirsty today. I have drunk from many other wells this week, some good, some bitter, but none satisfying. Give me a drink of the water of Your Spirit.

Discussion:

1. What is your favorite thirst-quenching drink? Why?

2. Can you recall times in your life when you have gone to the wells of success or other's opinions to quench your emotional thirst? Explain how that did or didn't satisfy your thirst.

3. During your coaching career, what lessons have you learned about paying too much attention to other people's opinions?

The Final Word

As coaches, we are continually evaluated by parents, newspapers, coffee shop talk, booster meeting opinions, media links, state and local prep editorials, etc. We have a lot of input as to our performance.

A fascinating story unfolds in the Bible beginning in Isaiah 36. The King of Assyria with an army of 185,000 invades Israel and is ready to destroy the city of Jerusalem. The King of Assyria, a guy by the name of Sennacherib, sends a threatening message to the King of Israel beginning with these words, "The King of Assyria says..."

When the King of Israel, Hezekiah, reads the message from Sennacherib, he is intimidated and sends a message to the prophet Isaiah which begins with these words, "This is what Hezekiah says . . ."

When Isaiah reads the message from Hezekiah, Isaiah the prophet says, "This is what the Lord says..."

Here's the point. Who gets the last word in our lives? To whose voice do we listen? The newspapers? Parents? Or do we hear clearly, "This is what the Lord says..." And what does God say? The Bible is what God says. Read His Word, and you will know "This is what the Lord says..."

Lord, there are lots of other 'says so's' in my life. Isn't that what Facebook is all about? May I go to Your Word for the real say so for my life. I choose Your opinion of me over all the others.

Discussion:

1. Have you ever felt unduly influenced or even intimidated by what parents or boosters have said to you or about you?

2. Read Psalm 27. What does it say about those who oppose us?

3. Do you have a regular time in your schedule where you can hear what God is saying to you by reading the Bible?

In Our Midst

The coach stood in the middle of his team in the locker room before taking the field. He looked each of them in the eye and spoke from his heart. What a coach says in those moments can make all the difference in the team's performance. A coach's words can take a team from fear to courage in an instant.

After Jesus' resurrection, the disciples were very uncertain about their future. In fact, they were fearful. Were they next to be nailed to a cross? What were they to do now?

"On the evening of the first day of the week, when the disciples were together with the doors locked for fear of the Jews, Jesus came and stood in their midst and said, 'Peace be with you!' After He said this He showed them His hands and side. The disciples were overjoyed when they saw the Lord."(John 20:19-20)

Fear one moment. Joy the next. The difference? Jesus came and stood in their midst.

Lord, I ask You today to come and stand in our midst. Come and stand in the middle of my heart, in the midst of my insecurities, fears, and uncertainties. Come and stand in the middle of this classroom, in the midst of this team, in the midst of my family. Even if the door of my heart is locked, come on in.

Discussion:

1. Imagine yourself in the room with the disciples. The door is locked for fear of the Jews. What might be going on in your mind?

2. Have you ever felt fearful or confused in your life when someone important to you left or made you feel alone? Would you mind sharing about that?

3. Imagine Jesus standing in this room right now. How would His presence make you feel? Is He here with you? (read Hebrews 13:5)

Not Fast Enough

Many years ago a long-time invalid joined a group of other fellow sufferers gathered at a pool in Jerusalem. The story goes that an angel would sometimes descend to the pool and stir the waters. Whoever got into the water first, got healed. The trouble was the 38-year invalid could never get to the pool first. Sometimes he was second; other times he got there in the top five, but he was never first.

He just couldn't get there fast enough.

Then one day Jesus came along and asked him a simple question, "Do you want to be healed?" The man explained to Jesus, "Sir, I have no one to put me into the pool when the water is stirred up, but while I am coming, another steps down before me." (John 5:7) To which Jesus replied, "Arise, take up your pallet and walk." The man immediately picked up his pallet and walked.

Like the invalid, we often run out of resources. Our reasoning, our intellect, and our own experience just aren't enough. We can't get to the pool first. What the invalid needed, as do we, is to look beyond our resources, the way we have been trying to do it for so long, and invite Jesus into the mix. The man didn't need to get into the pool. He needed to get to Jesus.

Lord, I confess I look to my resources first. I look to my experience or the advice of my friends. May You be my first line of defense, my first resource. I put You first in line.

Discussion:

1. Imagine yourself by the pool of Bethesda. The pool stirs, and you hear the crowd rush for the pool. You hear the joyful cry of the guy who made it first. How would you feel if you were NOT that guy?

2. Share a time you felt you had no more resources. What did you do?

Penetrations

The word penetration is used a lot by basketball announcers to describe players slashing through the defense and penetrating for layups or short jump shots. The ability to pierce the barrier of the defense is critical to achieve success on the hardwood.

Similarly, the media applauds defensive linemen for their ability to "penetrate" the offensive line and get into the backfield to make tackles or just disrupt the offensive flow.

God says the same thing about His Word. He says the Bible is "living and active and sharper than any double-edged sword. It penetrates even to the dividing of the soul and spirit, joints and marrow and is able to judge the thoughts and intentions of the heart." (Hebrews 4:12)

God's Word penetrates. It gets into the backfield of our hearts. It can judge our real motives, desires and intentions. It doesn't sound like a lot of fun, does it? But we are better off being honest with God about our real issues than playing games with Him.

Give God's Word a chance. Suit it up. Read it. Let it do its work in your life. Let it get past all your pretense and game playing and get to your deepest thoughts.

Lord, help me live my life out in the open. No pretense. No pretending. Nothing under the rug or in the closet. Expose my heart to your Word on a daily basis. Penetrate and heal.

Discussion:

1. Name the best defensive player you have watched who could penetrate the offensive line or penetrate the defense on the basketball court.

2. Share a time when God's Word penetrated your heart.

Drafted

NFL draft day! A big day for a lot of young men who hope to become part of an NFL team. For many, it would be the fulfillment of a lifelong dream. High prices would be paid for the services of these young men. Some would become millionaires overnight.

There is another draft day that happens every day. It is the day that anyone who puts their faith and hope in what Jesus has done on the cross gets drafted. The Bible uses the word adopted.

"In love, He chose us to be adopted as His sons through Jesus Christ by His pleasure and will." (Ephesians 1:5)

Imagine God stepping up to the microphone and saying, "Team Jesus picks ____!" Put your name in the blank!

Drafted by God, not to be on His team but to be His sons. Chosen to be a son. And unlike the NFL draft which selects only the fastest and the best, God adopts by His grace. He chooses us because He loves us regardless of our 40-yard dash time or our goodness or badness. He wants us just because He loves us.

So if you watch an upcoming draft, let it remind you that God has drafted you to be in His family, and you get way more than just a million dollar salary! (read Ephesians 1:3-14)

Lord, I am honored to be drafted by You, not just to be on Your team, but to be in Your family. Thanks for picking me. Wow! You have chosen me!

Discussion:

1. Imagine you have entered the draft and it is draft day. How would you feel waiting for the phone call to inform you that you have been drafted?

2. First John 3:1 says you are a child of God. What difference does it make that you are God's child and not just His creation?

Peanut Shells

There three ways to take in a baseball game: listen to the radio, watch it on TV, or go to the game in person and advantages and disadvantages to each. If you listen to the radio, you can hear the commentary of Marty Brenneman. If you watch it on TV, you get live action plus the comfort of home. Go to the ballpark, and you can throw the peanut shells on the concrete which you can't do at home! I choose option three, the ballpark.

Nothing beats being there! Nothing beats live action.

There will come a day when we will finally be at the game, a day we are face-to-face with Jesus.

"Dear friends, now we are children of God, and what we will be, has not yet been made known. But we know that when He appears, we shall be like Him, for we shall see Him as He is." (1 John 3:2)

Life with Jesus is good now, but there will come a day when it will get better. There is much about heaven we may not know or understand, but the best part is that we will see Jesus face-to-face. And we can probably throw the peanut shells on the ground there too!

Next time you listen to a baseball game on the radio or watch it on TV, remember there will come a day when we will be there. That will be sweet!

Lord, I look forward to being in heaven with You someday. For now, help me to enjoy being Your kid, but don't let me forget where my real home address is.

Discussion:

1. Which of the three options would you choose for experiencing an athletic event: radio, TV, or live?

2. What makes being at the game so great?

3. What are you most looking forward to about heaven?

Soccer or Football?

Soccer versus football. There are many similarities between the two sports. In some countries, although spelled differently, the names of the two sports (futbol and football) even sound the same.

If you watch the two games, however, you quickly realize that although they have much in common, they are very different.

Religion versus relationship. There are a lot of similarities between the two. Both refer to trying to connect with God. Someone defined religion as man's best attempts to reach God. It's like trying to long jump across the Grand Canyon. You may be an excellent long jumper, but you will end up in the same place that the not-so-good jumpers end up, at the bottom of the Grand Canyon.

Relationship, however, is God reaching down to humankind in the person of Jesus Christ. That's an entirely different ball game. Religion is trying. Relationship is trusting.

Paul said this in Romans 3:28 "For we maintain that a man is justified by faith (relationship) apart from observing the law (religion).

Jesus said in John 14:6, "I am the way, and the truth, and the life. No man comes to the Father except through me."

Football versus soccer. Religion versus relationship. Close, but a world of difference. It is the difference between knowing about God and knowing God.

Lord, I want to know You, like know you as a close friend. Like a father. I want a relationship with You. I am tired of trying to reach You on my efforts.

Discussion:

1. Share your preference for soccer or football and explain your choice.

2. Do you feel you have a relationship with God through Jesus or are you more in a religion mode?

False Starts

One sound that track coaches do not like to hear is the second shot from the starter's pistol indicating someone has false started and is now disqualified from the event.

No second chances.

I am glad God does not run life like a starter at a track meet. I have false started on many occasions. I have lost my temper with athletes, not believed the best of my wife, been jealous of other's success, and the list goes on. There have been many false starts in my life.

"In Him, we have redemption through His blood, the forgiveness of sins, by the riches of God's grace that He lavished on us with all wisdom and understanding." (Ephesians 1:7-8)

Have you false started recently? God says to us," Get back in the blocks! Let's try this again." Forgiveness is a great thing. It is beginning again. It is progress, not perfection. It is the sheer, incredible grace of God in Christ.

Lord, yes, I have false started today and deserve to be out of the race. I accept the second and third and fourth chances You give. I accept Your forgiveness and am ready to get back in the blocks.

Discussion:

1. Share a time you witnessed an athlete being disqualified from a race because he or she false started.

2. How do you think the athlete felt who false started? How did the coach feel?

3. Share a major or minor false start you have experienced in your life. Did God put you back in the blocks?

First and 10

"First and ten!" The best words the offensive coordinator can hear over the PA system. They mean his team has made enough yardage to entitle them to another set of four downs and another attempt to make progress toward the goal line.

Allow me to put a little spin on that familiar phrase. First thing in the morning, spend ten minutes with God. First and ten. It is a great way to start the day. You begin your day connecting with God, and if the day begins that way, there is a great chance it will continue that way. Time with God before time with people.

"Very early in the morning, while it was still dark, Jesus got up, left the house and went off to a solitary place, where He prayed." (Mark 1:35)

If you are not already doing this, set your alarm ten minutes earlier tomorrow morning. Read the Bible for five minutes, (the Psalms or the book of John is a great place to start.) Then pray for five minutes. Pray for your family, your staff, your athletes, yourself, for all those counting on you and those you are counting on.

When you hear the announcer on Friday night, say, "First and ten!" let it remind you of the great opportunity we have to pray and read God's Word early in the morning.

Lord, this is a great idea! I want to try this. Would You meet me in those ten minutes? Would You speak to me as I read Your Word? Would You teach me to pray? See You in the morning!

Discussion:

1. What are some rituals people enjoy first thing in the morning?

2. Is morning usually peaceful or hectic for you?

3. Is it possible for you to adjust your schedule so you can have a first-and-ten time in the morning?

Take a LAP!

A great struggle many of us coaches face is taking our worth from our team's performance. If our team performs well on Friday night or Saturday afternoon, we feel we have permission to feel good about ourselves. If our team loses, our sense of worth can plummet.

In Matthew, John the Baptist has just baptized Jesus, and the game is on! Jesus puts on His "Kingdom of God" jersey and steps onto the playing field of His ministry. Up to this point, He has been training, getting ready for three years of ministry which will culminate in His death on the cross that will change the course of history.

To this point preceding his baptism, Jesus has done nothing of significance as far as we know: no sermons, no healings, no "Hail Mary" passes. Just as Jesus comes up out of the water after being baptized by John, God speaks to His Son. "This is my son whom I love. With Him, I am well pleased." Three things God says about His Son: You are my son, I love You, and I am proud of You.

May I suggest that God feels the same way about you as He feels about His Son. He loves you. God accepts you. He is proud of you. Regardless of how you performed in the last game. Irrespective of your team's performance.

So before you go on the field or court next time, take a LAP. Before the game begins, know you are loved, God accepts you, and He is proud of you.

Lord, I accept Your opinion of me. You love me, You accept me and You are proud of me. Might Your opinion be foremost in my heart.

Discussion:

1. Why do you think it was important for God to say this to Jesus?

2. Is there anyone in your life who has communicated to you that they are proud of you? Would you share that moment with the group?

76

Assurance

Just last week a football coach told me, "If we win that game, we have an assurance of home-field advantage through the playoffs."

Assurance is a great thing. However, there is one condition to this coach's having home-field advantage. He has to win that game, and he has to keep on winning in the playoffs to keep that position.

It would be good to have the assurance of some things that don't depend on our performance. Assurance that no matter what the situation, the outcome is guaranteed.

"Keep your lives free from the love of money and be content with what you have, because God has said, 'Never will I leave you, nor will I ever forsake you.'" (Hebrews 13:5)

One thing you can be sure of; if you have invited the presence of Jesus into your life, He will never leave or forsake you, even if you lose the next game.

Lord, I receive Your assurance that You will never leave me. Others have let me down. I am glad I can count on You.

Discussion:

1. Did you ever coach or play in a game you had to win to advance to the playoffs or continue in the playoffs?

2. What are some things about which you feel reasonably sure?

3. Has anyone ever left or forsaken you? How did it make you feel?

4. How does it make you feel to know that God will never leave or forsake you?

Home or Away

Home or away? There's nothing like playing at home: the familiar field, familiar sounds, and the support of the home-town fans. As Dorothy said in "The Wizard of Oz," "There's no place like home!"

However, some coaches like playing away. There aren't as many personal distractions.

Paul felt a similar home or away tug when he wrote the following verse in 2 Corinthians 5:9.

"So we make it our goal to please Him, whether we are at home in the body or away from it."

Paul's home field was the right now, his present circumstances. Paul's away field was heaven. Paul decided that the real issue was not if he was here or there, but wherever he was, to please the Lord.

Coach, if you are playing at home this week, have pleasing God as your goal. If you are boarding a yellow dog (or a sweet charter with drop-down movie screens and reclining seats!) and playing away, have pleasing God as your goal.

Home or away. Grass or turf. Fair refs. Sorry refs. Ahead or behind. "Lord, help me please you."

Lord, this is my prayer, that I would please You regardless of the situations I am in, favorable or unfavorable. And by the way, we did have some bad refs last week!

Discussion:

1. Away games can be challenging. Describe one of the most difficult away game atmospheres in which you have ever played or coached?

2. Which do you like best, to play at home or away? Why?

3. How do you please God when you coach? What pleases God?

God Runs

A great story in the Bible is about a dad and a son. The son has been away from home for a long time, enough time to spend his share of the family inheritance his father had given him. The son finally comes to his senses and decides to return home, unsure of what his father's response might be.

"But while he was still a long way off, his father saw him and was filled with compassion for him; he ran to his son, threw his arms around him and kissed him." (Luke 15:20)

How far away was the son when the father saw him? He doesn't say for sure, but the father was watching. He was always on the porch, thinking "this might be the day my son returns!"

When the father sees his son, he sprints! Maybe he sees him over the crest of a hill and can tell just by the way his son walks. After all, he is his son. One thing is for sure. The father runs to his son.

The story is an excellent analogy of God's love for us. Life has a way of taking us far from home. Perhaps our own careless decisions have put a lot of space between God and us.

On the basis of this story, I can tell you that God will run to you. He will run so fast it will amaze you, but you have to take the first step. You have to get on the road with a broken heart. Next thing you know, God has run to you.

Lord, I am coming home. I have been away a long time. I think I see You running to me. I could use a hug.

Discussion:

1. Where do you think the father was when he saw his son down the road in the Luke 15 story?

2. Have you ever experienced a time when you felt God ran to you and forgave you for some pretty awful stuff?

The Clock

Clock management is critical in any game. Last Saturday, a radio announcer rebuked one of the playoff teams for wasting so much time in the final two minutes of play. A lot can happen in the last two minutes. You have to pay attention to the clock.

As I celebrated my 69th birthday in 2015, I realized afresh that time is running out, and I am smart to pay close attention to the time clock of my life.

A speaker at an FCA Camp in Michigan always began praying by saying, "This is a day that has never been and a day that will never be again."

Moses asked God to "teach us to number our days aright, that we may gain a heart of wisdom." (Psalms 90:12)

Life is lived a tick at a time. You may be in the first quarter of your life or the fourth quarter. You may think you are in the first quarter, but you are really in the fourth. You never know.

Lord, help me hear the clock of my life ticking. Keep me from just going through life with no sense of the eternal, no sense of urgency, just coasting. Help me live life on purpose, be intentional, and number my days.

Discussion:

1. Have you passed a milestone birthday in your life yet (the 30s, 40s, 50s)? How did it make you feel?

2. Why does life take on a more serious aspect when we reach those milestone birthdays?

3. What is something you can do today that you have been putting off because you always think you can do it tomorrow?

Wake up, Jesus!

Do you ever feel overwhelmed? Maybe it is that a stack of papers that seem to be shouting to you, "Grade me! Grade me!" Maybe it is the call you just received from the trainer telling you your starting guard won't be able to play Friday. Maybe it is a game situation. You are way behind, and it is early.

We have all felt overwhelmed, particularly in our season. Jesus' disciples felt that way when they were in a boat on a lake. A storm broke out, and suddenly there was more water inside the boat than outside. Making it worse, Jesus was asleep during all this mayhem! When they felt like they were going to drown, one of the disciples woke Jesus.

The best thing we can do in a storm is wake Jesus. The best thing we can do is get in touch with Him.

"He got up and rebuked the wind and the raging waters; the storm subsided, and all was calm. 'Where is your faith?' He asked His disciples." (Luke 8:24-25)

When life gets desperate, and we feel like we are going to drown, that's a perfect time to wake Jesus. We will still need to grade the papers, the guard still won't be able to play, and we may still be behind, but something happens in our heart when we wake Jesus and talk to Him.

Lord, I feel overwhelmed. I don't understand what is going on. Help my hope to be in You. Calm the storm raging in my heart.

Discussion:

1. Have you ever been in a boat, big or small, in a severe storm? How did you feel?

2. Why do you think Jesus was able to sleep? What is the last relational or emotional or spiritual storm you experienced? Were you quick to wake Jesus? What happened?

Jersey Name

A lot of teams wear jerseys with the name of the player on the back. I wonder what name Jesus would put on the back if he had a sports jersey. Would He put Jesus, or to be sure people got the picture, would he put Jesus/God? I guess there are a lot of names He could choose! Somehow I think Jesus might choose just Jesus. And maybe number two.

"Your attitude should be that of Christ Jesus, who being in the very form of God, did not consider equality with God something to be grasped but humbled Himself, taking the form of a bondservant, and being made in the likeness of men." (Philippians 2:5-7)

Jesus was God to be sure, but He never pushed his title or demanded recognition. I don't think He had God embroidered on His tunic.

Jesus always took the low place, the place of the servant. He washed His disciples' feet. He was probably last in line when He fed the 5000.

Lord, help me today to serve those I coach and teach and those who call me daddy or mommy. What can I do to help them?

Discussion:

1. Why do some teams put the names of players on the back of their jerseys? Why do some teams not put names on the backs of their jerseys?

2. Who is someone you know that is easily recognized but genuinely humble?

3. Have you ever been in a situation and felt like people would treat you differently if they knew who you were?

4. What is something you could do today to serve someone who is younger or has a less prestigious job than you?

Opposition

One of the great lessons athletics teaches is that the stronger, taller, faster, bigger person or team does not always win. The intangible ingredient called heart often determines who will be the winner.

Jesus once told a story about a king going out to battle. "Or suppose a king is about to go out to war against another king. Will he not first sit down and consider whether he is able with ten thousand men to oppose the one coming against him with twenty thousand?" (Luke 14:31)

The issue wasn't winning the war; it was merely having the willingness to oppose the other army. Often, just by having the courage to fight the other side victory comes, but even if not on the scoreboard, there is a success in opposing.

Coach, keep fighting the enemies in your life. Keep engaging the enemies that fight against our character. You may feel your army of ten thousand won't beat that army of twenty thousand, but you never know unless you fight. Like Rocky Balboa said, "Fighters fight"!

Lord, keep me fighting the battles of life! Keep me fighting for my marriage. Keep me fighting for my children. Keep me fighting for my team when so much seems to be against them. Help me be that one person who will fight for them.

Discussion:

1. Can you recall a time when you felt a team outmatched you? How did that situation end?

2. How can teams make adjustments when they feel overmatched?

3. Is there an opponent in your personal life you feel is overcoming you? A habit? A complicated relationship? A past mistake? Ask God to give you the courage to fight, and ask Him to get in the ring with you.

The Presentation

The presentation of trophies is always an exciting event! A trophy is awarded to the winning team and is immediately lifted overhead. It is a moment that team will never forget.

Over 2,000 years ago another kind of presentation was made. This time, a trophy was not presented. A person was offered. God the Father gave His only son, not as a trophy but as a sacrifice. Not to be put in a trophy case but to be nailed to a cross.

Romans 3:25 says, "God presented Jesus as the sacrifice for sin. God makes people right when they believe that Jesus sacrificed His life, shedding His blood."

God willingly gave Jesus as a sacrifice for our sin. God handed His only son over to a ruthless mob who enlisted the Roman army to nail Jesus to a cross. The world thought they were getting rid of a criminal. God was getting rid of sin.

Coaches, may I direct your attention, not to the center court, but to a hill outside Jerusalem and a man on a cross. Your attention to Him will make all the difference in your world.

Lord, thank you for presenting Yourself to die on a cross. Thank you for taking on my sin and enduring the penalty of a criminal so I could be forgiven and have eternal life.

Discussion:

1. Share a time when a team you played for or coached received a trophy? What was the occasion? How did you feel?

2. How does it make you feel to know that God presented Jesus as a sacrifice?

3. Has the sacrifice of Jesus become real for you? Have you accepted God's sacrifice of Jesus for your sin?

Last Minutes

We always remember the last minutes and seconds of great games. Consider the last minutes and the last hours of Jesus' life as it parallels yours.

6:00 a.m. Your alarm goes off. For Jesus, a rooster crows; He is betrayed for the second time in less than 12 hours; His eight-hour illegal trial continues.

8:00 a.m. Your first bell class arrives. Jesus receives 39 lashes with a whip in which are embedded pieces of bone and metal.

8:30 a.m. Your first bell class is half-way over. Jesus carries the cross to Golgotha. Jesus is weak from scourging and loss of blood; a stranger is enlisted to carry His cross.

9:00 a.m. Your second bell class arrives. Jesus' hands and feet are nailed to a cross; His shoulders dislocate as the bottom of the cross hits the bottom of the hole dug to stand up the cross.

12:00 noon. You eat your lunch in relative quiet in the teachers' lounge. For Jesus the sky goes black; God unleashes His wrath against sin on His Son for the next three hours.

3:00 p.m. The bell rings. Your school day is over, and you walk to practice. Jesus says, "It is finished" and breathes His last; Jesus' death pays for the sin of the world. Game over. Paid in full.

Lord, may I always be mindful of this day. May I never sleepwalk through the day and just count it up to religious history. I am so grateful.

Discussion:

1. How does it make you feel to look at the timeline of Jesus' death in comparison to the events of your day?

2. Have you allowed Jesus' death to pay for your sins, or are you trying to pay for them yourself by your good works?

Grandma Could Beat You!

Have you ever said something unkind to an athlete? Maybe it was said in anger or perhaps you were just trying to be funny but it came across as being sarcastic.

I did that Saturday at a meet at the University of Cincinnati. I remarked to one of our young runners that my grandmother could run faster! Not very kind! I tried to cover over my remark by saying nice things later on, but I knew I had been wrong.

Yesterday in church I was reminded of this verse. "Therefore if you are offering your gift at the altar and there remember that your brother has something against you, leave your gift there in front of the altar. First, be reconciled to your brother; then come and offer your gift." (Matthew 5:23-24)

So the next Monday during the early part of practice I pulled this young lady aside and said, "What I said Saturday about you not running faster than my grandmother wasn't very kind. I was wrong. Will you forgive me?"

She was quick to do that. She said that she hadn't even heard me say that, which helped a little!

I just hope this young lady never sees me run. She would be accurate to say that her grandmother could beat me!

Lord, may the words of my mouth give life to my athletes, not tear them down. Keep me from being sarcastic. If I am wrong, give me the courage to admit it and ask for forgiveness.

Discussion:

1. Have you ever said something unkind to an athlete and later had to apologize? Share that with the group.

2. Why do you think we as coaches get so upset with athletes for not performing well?

Submitting

Something in my stomach churned when the trainer said, "She can't run this weekend." Not only was I disappointed she couldn't run, but I also didn't like someone else telling me what I could not do.

Submitting to a trainer's decision is hard because I mistakenly think I know more than she does. Submitting to a trainer's decision is difficult because it reveals how proud I am and my total lack of humility. It is incredible that someone would know more about athletic injuries than me!

Romans 13:1 says, "Everyone must submit himself to the governing authorities, for there is no authority except that which God has established. The authorities that exist have been established by God."

Ouch! The issue for me is my failure to submit to God's authority, my inability to humble myself before others. I need to know that maybe, just perhaps, the trainer is more knowledgeable than I am, and God has placed her there for my good.

The issue for me is not a conflict with the trainer. It is a conflict with God.

Humility is hard, but I need to trust God that He is in control, and He is bigger than the trainer or me.

Lord, I take off my know-it-all pants! Help me submit to those in authority over me and trust You will use that for Your purposes in the lives of all those involved, especially mine.

Discussion:

1. Has a trainer ever informed you that an athlete will be unable to compete? How did you respond?

2. Why does it upset us when athletes cannot compete? Ask yourself "Why do I want so badly for this athlete to play?" Then ask yourself "why" again after each answer until you get to the root issue.

Overwhelming Odds

Sometimes our teams face overwhelming odds. The other team is too much speed, too much depth or too much strength.

A young king from the nation of Judah faced a similar situation. The young king's name was Asa. He had a pretty strong army, 580,000 warriors to be exact. That's a lot of warriors!

The only trouble was that the opponent, the Cushites, had almost twice that many warriors, more than 1,000,000, plus 300 chariots to make the numbers even more overwhelming!

The two nations faced each other on the battlefield, but before the battle broke out, Asa prayed this prayer: "Lord, there is no one like you to help the powerless against the mighty. Help us, O Lord our God, for we rely on You, and in Your name, we have come against this vast army. O Lord, You are our God; do not let man prevail against You." (2 Chronicles 14:11)

Asa was desperate. Asa prayed. He asked God to do for him what he could not do for himself. Asa knew there was no one like God to help when the odds are overwhelming. Asa knew there was no one like God to help when the odds are overwhelming.

Overwhelmed today? Ask God to get in the battle with you. By the way, the next verse says, "The Lord struck down the Cushites before Asa and Judah. The Cushites fled."

Lord, there is no one like You to help in the battle between the strong and those who have no strength. Fight for me. Keep me fighting when the odds are against me.

Discussion:

1. Who is the most overwhelming opponent you have ever faced?

2. Asa still had to fight the Cushites. We still have to do our part. What is your role in your battle? Who are your Cushites?

Negatives

Negative comments. Do you ever get those from a parent or one of your players? Perhaps an administrator? Even when you thought you did a good job, negative comments can dampen the hour.

That happened to me last week. I figured I was doing pretty well until I got some negative feedback from one of the athletes I was coaching. Bummer!

A couple of things helped pull me out of my downward spiral. First, I talked to my wife, Bobbie.

Second, a couple of Scriptures came to mind. One in 1 Peter 2 gave me some much-needed encouragement. "When they hurled their insults at Him (Jesus), He did not retaliate; when He suffered, He made no threats. Instead, He entrusted Himself to Him who judges justly."

First Corinthians 13 also came to mind: "Love does not take into account a wrong suffered. It does not hold grudges and will hardly even notice when others do it wrong."

I apparently have a lot to learn in this area of handling criticism. I do take hurts into account, and I do notice when others do me wrong. I very much felt like retaliating that morning. I had to ask God to step in and just change my heart, to give me His love for those people and me to not take things so personally.

Lord, keep me from retaliating and help me to entrust myself to You. You take care of the insults. I think You received a lot of them in Your lifetime.

Discussion:

1. Share a time when you were harshly criticized by a player or parent. How did you respond?

2. How do the above verses in 1 Corinthians or 1 Peter help in situations when we face criticism?

And One

She stopped on a dime and lofted a 3-pointer just outside the arc as she was fouled. The ball swished through the net. And then the whistle blew! Not only did she get three points. She got "and one."

And one. Not only is the shot good, but you get a bonus free throw and a chance to score another point.

The first chapter of Ephesians lists some incredible "and ones" for a person who has chosen Christ as Savior:

And one #1: We become sons and daughters. We become a "sit-next-to-God" kind of kid.

And one #2: We are redeemed by His blood, freed from our captivity and compulsion to sin by the death of Jesus.

And one#3: We understand His will; everything will one day be under the control of Christ.

And one #4: We are included in Christ. God has taken us in, and we are not outsiders anymore.

And one #5: We have received the Holy Spirit. The real deal. God lives in us.

Not a bad list of and ones! And, unlike the young lady's free throw which she may or may not make, these are all sure things.

Lord, thank you for being so generous and the bonuses I get from just having a relationship with You. Amazing!

Discussion:

1. Share a time when you were a part of an "and one" situation either as a spectator or participant.

2. Which of the above list of benefits in Ephesians is most meaningful to you? Why?

Oxygen Debt

Oxygen debt happens when muscles demand more oxygen than the lungs can provide. You may witness athletes with their hands on their knees or their head back, gasping for air.

Fortunately the body learns to adjust, and the lungs begin to supply more oxygen. It is called getting in shape!

As I was running earlier this past summer and experiencing a little oxygen debt myself, I thought of another debt I could never repay. No matter how hard I try or how sincere I am, I can never repay the debt of sin in my life.

Fortunately for us all, there is one who paid that debt for each of us.

"God made Him (Jesus) who had no sin to be sin for us, so that in Him we might become the righteousness of God." (2 Corinthians 5:21)

On the cross, Jesus Christ took the sin debt I owed and gave me His rightness in exchange. Sweet deal!

The next time you see an athlete going into oxygen debt and gasping for air, or you are experiencing that yourself, think of the one who died to pay an even greater debt, your sin and mine.

Lord, thanks for paying my oxygen debt of sin, something I could never pay myself. Without You, I would be gasping for life. I receive the righteousness of Christ as a gift.

Discussion:

1. Coach, when was the last time you experienced oxygen debt yourself?

2. Have you ever experienced other debt in your life? Maybe a school loan or a debt of gratitude to someone?

The Possession Arrow

The direction of the possession arrow during a basketball game is critical. Located on the scorer's table, the arrow points in the direction of the team that will be awarded possession the next time the arrow calls for a jump ball. It alternates to the other team after one team has had the call in its favor. In a tightly contested game, the possession arrow has a significant impact on the game's outcome.

Sometimes the possession arrow is in your favor; sometimes it is not. There is one possession arrow that is always pointing in your favor, however. In fact, it is looking at you!

One of the first books in the Bible says this, "For you are a people holy to the Lord your God. The Lord, your God, has chosen you out of all the people on the face of the earth to be his people, His treasured possession." (Deuteronomy 7:6)

God's possession arrow is always pointing in your direction. You are a treasure to God. You are a person of great value in the sight of God, bought at the cross with the price of His Son's death, and the arrow never switches to the other team. It is always pointing to you. After all, the arrow is on His table!

It may be a while before you see another basketball game, but when you do, and you see the possession arrow on the scorer's table, let it remind you that you are God's treasured possession!

Lord, thanks for choosing me. Thank you that the arrow of Your favor is always on me because of Your great grace.

Discussion:

1. Can you recall a game when the possession was in your favor, and that direction made a difference in the outcome of the game?

2. God's possession arrow is always pointing in your direction. Read Romans 8:31-39. What truths do you see that make you feel like a treasured possession of God?

Buckwheat Pancakes and Molasses

At the kitchen table, Coach Sweatsalot devoured the headlines as he sipped his Saturday morning coffee before heading to the stadium. "What a game!" he mused as he read the account of his team's come-from-behind victory over a larger and favored school. The words of the newspaper account were like buckwheat pancakes drenched with molasses!

As coaches, we can feed off newspaper accounts that celebrate our victories. The words sink deep into our hearts and affirm our worth.

However, unless we win every game, or every match, or every race, there might be some newspaper accounts that are not so kind or are perhaps just absent.

Jesus made a very intriguing statement concerning what feeds our minds. He said in the sixth chapter of John, "Just as the living Father sent me, and I live because of the Father, so the one who feeds on Me will live because of Me." (John 6:57)

The dictionary defines feed: "to become nourished, or satisfied or sustained as if by food."

Who or what will I feed off today? Newspaper accounts? Social media? Parents' opinions? Or Jesus and His Word?

Lord, give me more of an appetite for Your Word and less of an appetite for the reviews and opinions of others. Let me be more eager to open Your Word than I am to open my computer on the day after a game.

Discussion:

1. Share an account when the opinions of a newspaper article or the words of a prominent sports figure encouraged you? Discouraged you?

2. Do you have a regular time when you feed on God's Word or is it like a getting a snack from the vending machine?

Protection

Michael Orr starred in the movie *The Blind Side*. From his left tackle position, he gave what every right-handed quarterback needed, protection.

The Bible says God gives us protection today: I Peter 1: 3-4 talks about God's protection. It says that we are ". . . protected by God's power . . . "

Jesus prayed in John 17:11 "Holy Father, protect them by the power of Your name..." Later in the same chapter, Jesus prays, "My prayer is not that you take them out of the world but that you protect them from the evil one."

So from what does God keep you safe? Bad stuff. The big left defensive tackle of discouragement waiting to tackle you is evil. Jesus prays that God would protect you from evil.

Lord, protect me from evil. I get so caught up in what is going on down the field of my life that I don't even see evil bearing down on me. Thanks for having my back. And no look-out blocks!

Discussion:

1. Did you ever see the movie *The Blind Side*? What did you think?

2. Has a circumstance in life ever blindsided you? Share what happened.

3. Share a time you knew God protected you from some event which could have been very harmful to you.

Football and Fish

Bobby Bowden, the great football coach from Florida State, went on a weekend getaway with his wife early in his career. They stayed in a cabin, and the first night found both of them on the deck of their cabin looking at the stars.

Bobby's wife looked at Bobby and asked him, "Bobby, do you love me more than football?" A long silence. Stunned by Bobby's lack of quick response, his wife, blurted out, "Bobby, surely you don't have to think long about that answer, do you?" Deep in thought, Bobby was startled by his wife's voice. "Oh, I'm, sorry honey. I just didn't know if you meant college football or high school football."

After His resurrection, Jesus asked Peter a penetrating question just after He helped Peter and his boys catch a huge load of fish. They had just finished breakfast. Jesus looked at Peter and asks, "Simon son of John, do you truly love me more than these?"

I think that "these" in Jesus' question to Peter are the fish. Peter is a fisherman. He loved to fish, but did he love Jesus more than he loved the fish? That's the question.

Jesus is asking that we love Him more. We all love our sports. We love the game, and we love those we coach. If we didn't, we wouldn't be coaching. Jesus asks us to love Him more.

Lord, You know I love coaching. I just always want to love You more. That is so freeing for me. I don't have to give up coaching to love You. I just want to love You more than any game I ever coach, even if it is a state championship game!

Discussion:

1. Has there ever been a time in your life when your spouse might have felt that you loved your sport more than him or her?

2. How can we protect ourselves against loving our sport more than our spouses?

Now!

As coaches, we have to make a lot of critical decisions quickly. We have to decide which play to call, who to put in the game, and what pitch to call for the next batter.

Jesus was good friends with a woman named Martha, her sister Mary and their brother Lazarus. When Jesus heard of Lazarus's illness, instead of hurrying over, He waited two more days.

By the time Jesus arrived at Bethany, Lazarus had already been dead four days. Martha was perhaps a little perturbed with Jesus when He finally arrived, and in a "thanks a lot" tone said to Jesus, "Lord, if you had been here my brother would not have died." Jesus said to Martha, "Your brother will rise again."

Martha replied, "I know he will rise again in the resurrection at the last day." Jesus said to her, "Martha, I am the resurrection and the life." (John 11:24)

Jesus wanted Martha to see that He is the God of the now, not just the last day. He wanted to be the God of her "now."

Jesus wants to help you with whatever is your now: a stack of papers, projecting about the first-round playoff game, or a not so kind remark you made to your spouse just as you walked out the door this morning.

Lord, help me with the thoughts that swirl in my head. Be the God of my now. Take away anxiety and give me peace. Take away regret and give me hope. Take away anger and give me love.

Discussion:

1. What is the most critical, immediate decision you have ever had to make in an athletic contest?

2. What is the most pressing issue in your life now?

The Pulling Guard

If you are the tailback and running a sweep around the end, there is probably nothing as comforting as seeing big number 68 in from of you. The pulling guard. He is going to go before you and take out any would-be tacklers.

As Moses was ending his career as the leader of the nation of Israel, the nation was finally on the verge of crossing the Jordan River and getting into the Promised Land, a land they had been waiting for for 40 years. Moses said this to encourage the people.

"The Lord your God Himself will cross over ahead of you. He will destroy these nations before you, and you will take possession of their land. The Lord Himself goes before you and will be with you; He will never leave you nor forsake you. Do not be afraid; do not be discouraged." (Deuteronomy 31: 5, 8)

For the nation Israel, big number 68 was God Himself. God would go before them and clear other countries out of the way. For you and me, that same big number 68, God Himself, wants to go before us, into the unfamiliar, into that which would make us afraid or discouraged. God intends to go before you into that broken relationship, into that addiction, into that habit of anger and make a way.

Before you. With you. In you. God wants you to experience Him today.

Lord, I need Your help to clear the way for me today. I have been angry already, and it is barely 10:00. I have blamed others and judged their motives. Help me see the blank places in my heart that only You can fill.

Discussion:

1. Can you recall any pulling guards or fullbacks who did a great job to make a way for others to run the ball?

2. In what area of your life do you need God to run some interference?

No Instant Replay

The head referee turned on his mic. "After further review, the calling on the field stands. Ball fumbled on the one-yard line." Instant replay. It gives meet officials and even those somewhere in New York a chance to look at the situation again for a definitive call.

Even though almost all sports have incorporated instant replays, there is one domain in which there are no reviews.

God doesn't do instant replays. He doesn't dig up the past. Confessed sins are forgiven and forgotten with no finger-wagging and no lectures.

God says in Jeremiah 31:34, "Their sins and lawless deeds I will remember no more."

Paul stated in Philippians 3:13-14: "Forgetting what lies behind, and reaching for what lies ahead, I press on for the upward call of God in Christ Jesus my Lord."

The next time you hear a referee call for a timeout to review a play, thank God that He doesn't discuss your past. The calling on God's field will always stand. FORGIVEN!

Lord, thank you for not making a tape of all my past. All the times I yelled at the ref and my wife! Make me as good a forgetter as You. Thanks for washing away my sins on the cross.

Discussion:

1. Do you like having instant replay available, or do you think the referee's call should always stand?

2. Share a time when you have been on the receiving end of a bad call from a ref.

Concerned or Controlling?

I was not able to be at practice yesterday. I was in Lexington at an FCA Marriage Getaway where I was supposed to be learning about how better to encourage my wife. Instead, I found myself fretting. I worried for some time about the workout the track team was supposed to do. "Do they know what time they are to workout? Do they understand what the workout is?"

Control. I am not a control freak, but I'm a nine on a scale of one to ten! Perfectionism also is a part of this mode. I don't have much capacity to give myself grace or give it to anyone else.

What I need to do is learn to be concerned without being controlling.

I know these verses in my head, but I suffer from blockage getting them to my heart. Proverbs 3:4 and 5 say, "Trust in the Lord with all your heart, and lean not on your own understanding. In all your ways acknowledge Him, and He will make your paths straight."

Psalm 37:7 says, "Refrain from anger and turn from wrath; do not fret..." I am an excellent fretter. I need to be a better truster.

Maybe by the time I am 70, I will learn these things! Oops! I just turned 70 two months ago! I will extend the deadline to 80!

Lord, life for me is like one big funnel with me at the bottom. I like everything to flow through me, to have my hands on every decision and to have people ask my advice often. I give up that desire to control everything to You. Here, You call the plays.

Discussion:

1. Are there coaches you have played for whom you would consider being high control?

2. Are control and perfectionism an issue in your life? If so, in what areas do you see that played out?

The Big Three

Football coaches enter most games with three big things they must do to win the game and also three big things they must avoid not to lose the game. The top three big things to avoid might include turnovers, penalties and giving up the big play.

Jesus had some things to say about three big issues to avoid in life in a story He told as He was teaching a crowd of people around the Sea of Galilee. He was telling a story about a farmer who sowed some seed, the different places the seed could land and the possible outcomes based on the various places the seed might land.

"Still others, like seed sown among thorns, hear the word, but the worries of this life, the deceitfulness of riches, and the desires for other things enter in and choke the word, making it unfruitful." (Mark 4:18-19)

The thorn that chokes the word in me most often is my desire for other things, specifically an inordinate desire to win. There is nothing wrong with winning; as coaches, we love to WIN! But is that desire choking out God's activity in my life? Is that desire cutting off the supply of spiritual oxygen to my heart?

What can we do? I need to ask God to help me pull up those thorns of desire from my heart, and give me more of a desire for Him, His Word, and His people than for the numbers on a scoreboard or a stopwatch.

Lord, these thorns of desire are pesky. I thought I pulled up those last week and now here they are again. I pull them up as best as I can. Guard my heart against those thorns that battle for places in my heart.

Discussion:

1. What is your usual game plan?

2. Which of the three thorns bothers you the most, worrying, being deceived, or desires for other things?

Grace Wins

It was the strangest scoreboard I had ever seen and the most bizarre game I had ever witnessed.

Whenever a score went up on the left side, the score went up one more on the right side. No matter how many points the team on the left scored, the team on the right was always ahead by one point! I was sitting in a remote part of the gym and couldn't make out the names of the two competing teams. At halftime, I walked down from my seat and peeked in the door at floor level. The name on the left said Sin. The side on the right said Grace.

"...But where sin increased, grace increased all the more." (Romans 5:20)

It seemed no matter how many points the Sin team scored, Grace was always ahead.

There might not be a scoreboard like this in real life, but the truth is real. God's grace is always ahead of our sin. Corrie Ten Boom said, "No hole is deeper, that God's love is not deeper still."

You might feel like sin has put you in a deep hole, that the number on the sin side of the scoreboard needs a place for three digits rather than just two. Whatever the issue, whatever the sin, God's grace will always be up by one!

Lord, I feel the sin side of the scoreboard is maxing out. Wherever I go - home, school, the field—the numbers on the sin side keep mounting. I desperately need Your grace today.

Discussion:

1. Share a time in your life when it was a close game between sin and grace?

2. How have you seen God's grace in your life?

Put me in, Coach!

Freddy sat on the bench, craning his head in the direction of the coach. Today was his last game, his final chance to play. Seeing his career come to an end with under a minute to play, Freddy leaped to his feet, turned in the direction of the coach and yelled, "Coach, put me in!"

Jesus met up with a guy very similar to our young man on the bench. However, this guy was blind. His name was Bartimaeus. Jesus was leaving the city of Jericho when Bart hears that Jesus is passing by.

"When he heard it was Jesus of Nazareth, he began to shout, 'Jesus, Son of David, have mercy on me!' Many rebuked him and told him to be quiet, but he shouted all the more, 'Son of David, have mercy on me!' Jesus stopped and said, 'Call him.' So they called to the blind man, 'Cheer up! On your feet! He is calling for you.'" (Mark 10:47-49)

We get Jesus' attention when we call His name. When we call his name, He calls for us.

Be as bold as Bart to tell Jesus what you need. Maybe it is an emotional issue, a feeling of anxiety or rejection that has plagued you for a long time. Whatever it is, visible or not, just tell Jesus what you need.

Lord, I am calling on You. You know the turmoil of my heart, the unmet expectations. I ask You to heal me on the inside as much as You healed Bart on the outside.

Discussion:

1. Have you ever had a player approach you and ask you to put him or her in the game? How did that turn out?

2. If Jesus was passing by right now and asked you "What do you want me to do for you?" what would you say? What is your most significant need right now?

The Playoffs

Losing is never fun. It can bring forth emotion ranging from mild disappointment to outright despair. The deeper you go into the playoffs, the higher the expectations and the more deeply it hurts to lose.

"For whoever wants to save his life will lose it, but whoever loses his life for My sake will save it. What good is it for a man to gain the whole world, and yet lose or forfeit his very self?" (Luke 9:23-25)

Those are pretty high stakes! Losing your very self! And yet Jesus says that can happen if we attempt to preserve or guard our life above all else.

So I ask myself, "How do I try to save my life?"

I lose when I try to protect my own reputation or correct someone who might have misquoted the score of last year's game. There are any number of things I may do to protect my sense of worth and honor. At each of those moments, I lose.

I save my life when I give up control to Jesus for His sake, when I become more interested in His Kingdom than in my kingdom, when I become more interested in people who don't know Jesus than I am in people who don't know me, when I choose relationship with an athlete over the performance of an athlete. That's when I win.

Lord, I lose a lot in this contest for my soul. My protective self rises each time I feel threatened. May I allow other people to have their way, to give up pushing and shov- ing my way through the merging onramps of life. Forgive me for the countless ways I try to gain the whole world.

Discussion:

1. Are your emotions different when you lose a game in the regular season than when you lose a game in the playoffs?

2. Do any of the above scenarios describe you?

All Gone

The whistle blows, and you send your players to the sideline for a drink. Players grab the green bottles and squeeze the last drop out of them. Nothing left.

Hebrews 2:9 says, "But we see Jesus, who was made a little lower than the angels, now crowned with glory and honor because He suffered death so that by the grace of God He might taste death for everyone."

When Jesus died, He picked up the bottle of spiritual death and drank it all! Nothing left. The bottle of all our bitterness and lust and jealousy and anger and resentment. Jesus drank it all.

So we get a new bottle. The bottle of grace, and it never runs out. You can drink as long and as often as you need. You take a drink; God refills it. Nice bottle, huh!

We get the bottle of grace because Jesus drank the bottle of our sin.

Next time you are thirsty and take a drink, thank God for the bottle of grace we have in Jesus.

Lord, thanks for trading bottles with me. Thank you for tasting the cup of death for everyone. Thanks for the new bottle of grace which is so satisfying and quenches my deepest thirsts in life.

Discussion:

1. When you were an athlete, how did your coaches treat water breaks? Did they give them willingly or begrudgingly?

2. Is it hard for you to drink from the bottle of grace? Would you just rather be thirsty than receive something you don't deserve?

Second Chances

Dropped batons. False starts. Fouls at the takeoff board. Double fault serves. Called third strikes. All kinds of disasters can happen in the blink of an eye in spring sports, and I've committed my share of these miscues myself. I've dropped my share of batons: failed to communicate truth to my son.

Thankfully, most of these real-life scenarios are not fatal. I have another chance. I can try again to speak truth to my son. I can get up a few minutes early and have that so-needed time to be still with God before walking out the door to a very hurried world. I can say no to that meeting and choose to play Scrabble with my wife. I can learn from two mistakes and not do it a third time. I can appreciate the opportunities God gives me and be grateful for the chances I have.

Paul says in Philippians 3:12, "Not that I have already obtained all this or have already been made perfect, but I press on to take hold of that for which Christ Jesus took hold of me. Brothers, I do not consider myself yet to have taken hold of it. But one thing I do: Forgetting what is behind and straining toward what lies ahead, I press on toward the goal to win the prize for which God has called me heavenward in Christ Jesus."

Lord, thank you for second chances. Thanks for another turn at bat, another race to run, another serve to hit. Help me learn when I can, but please forgive me when I fall short.

Discussion:

1. Share a time you committed an athletic miscue (dropped baton, fumbled ball, missed the crucial free throw, etc.)

2. How did your coaches react when you committed those mistakes?

Laces

Laces. Laces on a football give the quarterback an excellent grip on the ball, and laces on a baseball give the pitcher the grip he needs to throw that great curveball, but laces do more than just give a player a tight grip on the ball he or she is throwing. Laces hold the ball together. Without laces, the ball flies apart in all directions.

Our lives have laces too, and sometimes it seems those laces start to loosen and life begins to unravel.

Colossians 1:17 says of Jesus "In Him, all things hold together." Jesus holds everything together.

He holds my calf together when I am on the run and I feel it start to pull.

He holds my emotions together when I feel anxious before a meet.

He holds my heart together when my affections could fly in all directions.

Jesus holds life together for me. Jesus provides the laces of my life.

So today if life seems like it is about to fly apart and you need something to hold you together, Jesus can do that. He can hold you together; He can keep your team together; He can hold your marriage together. Jesus can keep everything together.

Lord, life seems to unravel for me at times. When I see the laces of my heart start to unwind, help me to remember that You hold all things together.

Discussion:

1. Have you ever played with a ball when the laces were loose or unraveling? How did it impact your performance?

2. Share a time when life began to unravel for you. What held you together? Or did you fly apart?